HENRY SUSO
Saint and Poet

Nihil Obstat: HENRICUS FRANCISCUS DAVIS, B.A., D.D.

Imprimatur: ✠ HUMPHREY BRIGHT, Vicarius Capitularis.

Birmingamiae, die 28a februarii anno 1947.

B. HENRY SUSO

Fra Angelico
[National Gallery

HENRY SUSO

SAINT AND POET

A Study

by

S. M. C.

(Of the English Congregation
of Saint Catherine of Siena)

BLACKFRIARS : OXFORD

FIRST IMPRESSION   1947

PRINTED IN GREAT BRITAIN
BY WESTERN PRINTING SERVICES LTD., BRISTOL

FOREWORD

When the smoke-cloud which hung for six years over Europe lifted at last, the world with frightened eyes looked out over the havoc and ruin which had been wrought. Even those who have suffered least can see, often from their own doors, the rubble of bomb-blasted wreckage. For many, nights of vigil brought long, solemn thoughts. God, in his mercy, had driven his children back to those vigils, fasts and other privations which had been for so long discarded as outworn relics of medievalism, sufferings which the saints have run to embrace.

People may shrink from tales of suffering, whether self-inflicted or sent by God. Yet if the path to such suffering had not been lost, this other, ghastly and inhuman as it was, would never have fallen on mankind.

Six hundred years ago, Blessed Henry Suso journeyed backwards and forwards through the Rhineland and Ruhr, now so much of it rubble. He preached to the folk of his time by word, and yet more by the unspoken word of his life. His message is as pertinent to the world now as it was then. The very human weakness of his life, his shrinking from the sufferings which his will embraced, brings encouragement.

He is pre-eminently a saint for our own times, for he embodies the spirit of patience, humility and love of the Cross, which we also must learn, every one of us, if this shattered world is to be rebuilded aright.

This is what our Lord himself told his servant:

Divine Wisdom: Listen to the reason why I try my servants in so many ways; and what I am about to tell you, impress deeply on your heart.

I dwell in a soul as in a paradise of delights, and so I cannot

v

permit her to find any joy apart from me. And, since I wish to possess her in chastity and purity, I encompass her with thorns and enclose her in adversity, so that she cannot escape from my hands. I sow her path with sorrow and anguish, so that she cannot rest in base and created things, and so that she may place all her happiness in the depths of my divinity. The reward that I give such souls for the least suffering that they bear is so great that were the hearts of all worldlings united in one they would be overwhelmed by it. The way of the Cross is not new, it has always been. I have willed that rare and sublime things should be difficult of attainment, and that virtue should demand weariness and sweat. If this way is displeasing to the soul, if she wishes to abandon it, to estrange herself from me, let her go! I have created her free and I will not force her. Only too true is the word of the Gospels: " Many are called but few are chosen."

Again:

The Cross possesses such power and strength that, whether they will or no, it attracts, draws, and ravishes those who carry it. How many there are who would have been damned if I had not crucified them. It is a greater thing to preserve patience in adversity than to raise the dead to life. Patience is a living sacrifice, breathing a delicious perfume in the presence of my Divine Majesty. It is a sacrifice so necessary to the glory of the soul, that I would draw crosses and trials from nothingness rather than deprive my dearest friends of them. It is true that the way of the Cross appears narrow and wearisome, but it leads those who follow it to the gates of heaven, to the glory of the saints, to the triumph of the martyrs; and then the sufferers in the joy of their victory will sing to the Lord a new canticle in which the angels themselves cannot join, for they have never carried the Cross.

CONTENTS

PRAYER OF BLESSED HENRY SUSO

My Jesus, wounded and abandoned, grant by the merits of thy unshakable patience, that in prosperity and adversity I may remain always equable, calm and unmoved, as if I were nailed with thee to the Cross. Fasten to the Cross the powers of my soul, above all my understanding and will, in such a way that I understand, and love nothing but the Cross, and that I am unable ever to seek the love of the world and the pleasures of the body. Let there be no part in me which, in its own way, does not meditate on thy passion and death, and which does not most faithfully represent thy most lovely passion. Amen.

ACKNOWLEDGEMENTS

Grateful thanks are due to Messrs. Burns, Oates and Washbourne and to the Superior of the London Oratory, for permission to use Father Sebastian Bowden's *Autobiography of Blessed Henry Suso*. Grateful acknowledgement is also due to the Trustees of the National Gallery for permission to reproduce the picture of Bl. Henry Suso from the Altar Piece from the Church of San Domenico in Fiesole by Fra Angelico (*Frontispiece*). Among those who have helped with suggestions or in revising the MS. the writer wishes in particular to thank Fr. Walter Gumbley, O.P., and Fr. Sebastian Bullough, O.P.

CHAPTER I

HENRY

ON the feast of Saint Benedict, March the twenty-first, in the year 1290, there was born to the Swabian Count von Berg and Anna Suess, his wife, a son who was christened John, but who was later known as Henry.

In after years the Count used to wonder sometimes whether he had made a mistake in allowing the lying-in to take place in his new timber house on the outskirts of the little town of Uebenlingen instead of in the old castle on the hill which had been the cradle of his race; for the boy grew up entirely unlike the rest of the family. At its best it was not a happy household, for Count von Berg was a rough, difficult-tempered man, no worse probably than the general run of nobles of the period, but certainly no better. His wife was as gentle, patient and pious as he was the reverse; her saintliness annoyed her husband and he used to treat her very harshly.

As little Henry grew from babyhood to boyhood he became a further source of irritation to his father, for every day he grew more entirely like his mother. The other lads spent their time in hunting, hawking and the exercises of the tiltyard, but Henry found his pleasure in going on pilgrimage with his mother from church to church. Sometimes they would cross the Lake into Constance and make their way through its narrow streets to the Cathedral, and after they had heard Mass they would kneel together at the foot of the great rood, in that place where, many years later, the Countess was taken with her last illness.

All this made the Count furiously angry, and he would rail at his wife, saying that Henry was no son of his, but a puling, priest-ridden fellow, more of a maid than any of his sisters, who were, after all, girls of spirit. Anna Suess held her peace, but she suffered nevertheless and Henry suffered in her suffering, for he loved her with all his heart.

Unable to change his wife's manner of life, von Berg would turn to his son to try the effect on him of mingled threats and blandishments; but it was all to no purpose and, as the years passed, the Count began to understand that, though Henry might make a name for himself in the ecclesiastical state, he was worse than useless as a young squire training in knightly exercises.

So he began to turn his thoughts in this new direction for, indeed, he had a large family, and a priest son was cheaper to educate than a soldier. He could not even find marriage portions for all his daughters; some must be nuns since the dowry was smaller. For once he would please his wife, and her favourite son should join her favourite Order of the Friars Preachers. The Priory in Constance was making a great name for itself; Henry might become a famous preacher in time; heaven knew he was fit for nothing else. The outcome of these musings was that in the year 1303, when the boy was just thirteen years old, his father took him into Constance to offer him to the friars there.

There was little regret in Henry's heart as he followed his father down the village street. He was going to miss his mother bitterly, but as for the remainder of his family, with the possible exception of that young sister who was going into a convent shortly, he had never had much in common with them. He was vaguely sorry for the girl, who merely acquiesced in the future planned for her, whereas he was definitely glad for himself. Still, there were many convents where girls could have quite a pleasant time and really enjoy more freedom than if they stayed at home.

As for his beloved mother, Henry was glad that he had it for once in his power to give her real joy. He was not sorry either to think that he would no longer stand by helpless when his father was irritated with her; an irritation which

2

he never took the slightest pains to conceal. Henry suffered in her pain, and he had not yet learnt the secret of the alchemy by which she transmuted all bitter things to sweetness, by casting them into the sufferings of Christ. Because mother and son loved one another so dearly, she showed him the secret of her heart, her burning love for our Lord and his Blessed Mother. Though her secret was not yet his, because his mother confided in him Henry grew to love her ever more dearly; later his own experience taught him to find his strength in the same source. Perhaps love of his mother was the reason for Henry's changing his father's family name for hers, Suess; though this may have been done later and for another reason.

The journey from the village of Uebenlingen, on the outskirts of which stood the town house of the von Bergs—more like a medieval manor than a feudal castle—to the lakeside was not a long one, and there, at the quay, the Count's wherry was waiting for them. The boy paused for a moment to look west, over the dark green waters of the lake to the dream-lovely gothic pile of the priory, standing on the north-west bank just where the Rhine left it on its journey seaward.

There it stood, a grey building, its tracery as fine as lace work, framed in green lawns which stretched right to the water's edge. Behind, in the haze, lay Constance itself, an imperial city, sending members to the Imperial Diet, a cathedral city which owed allegiance to none but its own city council and the Emperor himself. It was an important trading centre too, for traffic from the Hansa towns of the north found its southern emporium at this upper end of the river. Behind the town and on either side rose hills covered in vine, olive and ripening corn framed in the blue of the sky.

Henry followed his father into the wherry and seated himself in the thwarts, trailing his hand idly in the deep green of the water.

3

As he followed von Berg into the precincts of the priory half an hour later, the boy knew that he was satisfied with the future planned for him. He had never been happy at home for, besides his perpetual anxiety for his mother, he loathed the noisy sports and the rough-and-tumble of life there. He loved quiet and beauty and his own dreams, and he felt that his aspirations would find their outlet in the Dominican Order. Besides, there was always the thought of his mother's joy.

Meanwhile Henry's father was speaking to the prior, making a formal application for his son's entrance to the novitiate, and arranging for the payment of certain sums for his keep and education. The business concluded, the boy knelt for his father's blessing, and was taken inside the enclosure to be handed over to the novice master.

A Dominican priory is a lovely place, and to Henry's beauty-loving soul the appeal was a strong one. It is built in the form of a quadrangle round a cloister garden. The church stretches the length of the north cloister. It is a large building with the choir screened in such a way that the devotions of the brethren cannot be seen by seculars. The chapter room opens off the west cloister, while the refectory is parallel to the south one. Above the refectory is the infirmary, while the dormitory is over the east cloister and its offices.

The dormitory was a replica of the cloister below, except that down either side there were compartments open to the central corridor, but divided from each other by partitions the height of a man. Elsewhere, there was a number of small rooms where the professors and the most promising students had the advantage of complete quiet. In these cells —whether compartments in the common dormitory, or separate rooms—the brethren might study, sleep, or pray.

In the first ages of the Order the friars slept fully dressed. At the signal given at midnight, all rose and recited the Little Office of the Blessed Virgin before her statue at the

4

end of the dormitory; beginning the first *Ave* as they left their beds. At the second signal all went to the church for matins, using the great breviaries which were chained to iron stands in the centre of the choir, facing right and left, so that a number could read from them at the same time.

Matins ended, those who chose remained behind for silent prayer until prime. From prime onward the day was divided between study, work and prayer until, with compline, the Deep Silence began in order that the closing hours of the day might be the more easily dedicated to study and contemplation.

There were other novices of Henry's own age and all went to school together. Though the new novice was very ignorant, his intelligence was much above the average, and so he was very happy during the two years that he spent in the grammar school. In addition to secular study, there were the novitiate lessons, choir chant, ceremonial and the constitutions of the Order. He soon became a favourite with his companions, for he was of a naturally sociable disposition, a good mixer, and congenial environment brought out his native charm of manner.

Neither was his life all prayer and study, for sometimes he was sent out as companion to a preacher, to follow him to the church where the sermon was to be delivered, there to sit on the pulpit steps. Or he might be sent with the brother who went to quest for food through the narrow streets of the town where the upper stories of the houses almost touched; streets crammed and jammed with the traffic of a great merchant city.

When he was fifteen he passed on to the school of arts, there to study logic, mathematics and rhetoric. There were ordinarily two lecturers appointed to each class of students; the master, or solemn lecturer who gave the morning lecture; in the afternoon, the cursor, or lector, gave the cursory lecture, a digest of the matter of the morning's lecture. Henry found the second of the two the more entertaining, and by this time he was on the look-out for entertainment.

He sat with his fellows on low benches at the master's feet and committed to memory the subject of the lecture. In the winter-time they brought in straw to wrap round their feet so that the biting cold might distract them less. There were few books and extensive notes could not be taken on tablets, so every day he was called up in his turn to make repetition of the morning lecture. The solemn weekly repetition was intended to fix the whole still more firmly in his mind.

After two years spent in arts, Henry passed on to philosophy. He knew that three years later he would begin the course in theology, and perhaps, if he passed his examinations well enough, he might be sent with the more brilliant students to the *Studium Generale* in Cologne.

Perhaps the piety of his childhood's days had resulted more from love of his mother than from love of God. Be this as it may, by the time that he reached philosophy there was very little of it left. Not that he was by any means a bad religious; even from a human standpoint he was too naturally fastidious to fall into the grosser forms of sin. In all probability his head was considerably turned by popularity; he enjoyed life, and he found that he could get a good deal of amusement out of it while still keeping the letter of the constitutions sufficiently well to avoid clashes with authority. His intellect was considerably above the average, and he was making his mark in school without taking any excessive pains with his work.

There were times, of course, when the memory of his mother's teaching, the narrowness of his own rather purposeless life, and a stirring within, which urged him to something more worthy of his vocation, became a real trouble to him. Conscience pricked him, and he used to see, without in the least desiring it, the ideal after which he had promised to strive. The artist in him was waking also and,

6

as he had no idea of this, he did not understand how to ignore the alternate moods of exhilaration and depression which at times took possession of him.

He was finding too, like so many others, that pleasures in their realisation are poor things compared to their anticipation. He loved pleasure and his better self found this love a prison in which, like a caged bird, he was held unable to fly to God. He knew that his life was unworthy of his high vocation as a friar preacher, and yet he was held back by the fear of suffering which he knew to be the price of complete surrender to God. And so he remained restless and ill at ease in the depths of his nature, his untamed heart vainly seeking peace; at all times feeling within himself the gnawing pain of self-reproach, and yet, until God should draw him irresistibly to himself, unable to take the step which he knew to be the only way to peace.

When these moods possessed him he became silent, morose, irritable. Then his companions would say laughing to one another that Brother Henry was in one of his black moods, and would leave him alone until, having stifled for a time the voice of conscience, he would return to them, his old, gay, laughing self.

And so the years passed until he reached his eighteenth birthday, a good-looking young man, fresh-complexioned, bright-eyed, and sanguine; a student who had been trained in the use of his faculties, full of potentialities for good or evil; a colt on which no man had yet ridden standing at the cross-ways.

CHAPTER II

THE BRIDE

THE spiritual process which we call conversion is in reality two things, not one. There is *aversion,* which is turning away from a life of sin, lukewarmness, or the inordinate love of any earthly object; and there is *conversion* properly so called, a turning to virtue, fervour and the love of God. Since it is twofold it may be actuated by one of two motives. A man may turn away from something ugly in order to lose sight of it, and then he must find something else to look at, for no one can remain facing a void. But this turning may be, not away from something, but towards something beautiful, and in this case one image has driven out another and there is no void. When the process we call conversion begins with aversion, then there is a void which must be filled; but if the first movement has been a turning towards God there is no void, for his love has driven out what formerly occupied the place which is his by right.

Friar Henry's conversion began after he had ended his two years' study of logic and had already been a year in the school of natural philosophy; and it began in aversion from the aimless, lukewarm life that he had been leading. What finally moved him no one knows; whether a vision of hell, or a sudden realisation of whither his present life was leading him. Whatever it was, the motive was powerful enough to determine him to make a complete break. So he began in earnest to empty his heart of creatures in order to give himself entirely to God.

In this way a void was created and, a void being an unnatural thing, a soul which has emptied itself of creature love is in an unnatural state until someone, God or the devil, takes possession of the house swept and garnished. It was not long therefore before his fellow students perceived that there was something unnatural about Henry.

" He has become good in an uncomfortable sort of way," they said to one another, as they watched him going about the house with eyes resolutely cast down and tightly closed lips. So, finding him an uncomfortable companion they kept away from him.

Neither was Henry any more natural and at ease within

himself than he was with his fellows. For a while all would go well and he would be happy in this more complete service of God, but such seasons of good cheer were followed by periods of depression and temptation. He would consider within himself that, after all, there had been nothing really wrong with the life he had been leading and so there could be no reason in making himself singular by trying to better it. Many good people contrived to get the best out of both worlds, and why should he set himself out to be different? At times these questions fretted him almost beyond endurance, for at the bottom of his heart he knew that for him the spiritual life must be all or nothing.

It was when these black moods fell on him that he felt that he could not face all that was entailed by a complete turning from tepidity, and so, to escape from the importunities of his conscience, he used to slip away in search of his fellow students, those young men with whom he had been until lately on such excellent terms.

He found them in the common-room or in the garden, and he hurried over to them, hoping to hear the old familiar greeting. But his hope was always dashed for, instead of comradely familiarity, after a half-hearted word or two they subsided into silent embarrassment. After all, what else could he expect? This Henry was a stranger to them; they had often speculated among themselves as to what had changed him, making him dull and heavy—in a word, dreadfully *good*—so that they felt shy and constrained in his presence. And he, for his part, after he had made a few awkward attempts to return to the old relations of comradeship soon gave up the attempt, for he discovered that he had quite lost the art of joining in their conversations, finding them tasteless and insipid, though he had, as yet, nothing of his own to offer in their place.

Presently his puzzled friends began to account for the change in their companion by remarking that, after all, he had always been different from other people, one never quite knew how to take him; though none of his many moods had lasted as long as the present one. But then he always went to extremes, and this new bee in his bonnet would eventually go the way of the rest. So, when he appeared among them, shy, awkward and ill at ease, they used to tease him, hoping that friendly ridicule might restore him to his normal delightful self.

"What are these strange ways you have taken to?" asked one.

"The middle path is the safest," added another.

"Your new-fangled notions will bring you to a bad end," said a third.

And so they talked and jested, while Henry, who had always been supersensitive and was still far from attaining a saving sense of humour, would look from one to the other in dumb misery. He had gone to these friends of his because, being sad, he wanted to become merry. But it was useless to seek help there, and he soon slipped away again, more depressed than ever. And as he sought solitude he used to murmur:

"My God, the best thing I can do is to keep away from everyone, for when I am alone there is nothing to grieve me."

This loneliness and depression probably arose from a variety of causes, some of them other than spiritual; for Henry was a genius and, until the creative gift finds its proper outlet, it brings a sensation of frustration and loneliness. Henry's genius was still pent up within and consequently a danger. But a far greater danger lay in the fact that his heart was void just when young manhood was in the first glow of its strength and power; and that in a century when the uprush of life was greater than we can even comprehend.

It was at this critical time that a beautiful thing happened to Friar Henry; he fell in love.

It happened one day when he was feeling more than

usually wretched that, the midday meal ended, he made his way to the choir and settled himself in one of the stalls in the lower right-hand side. To his right was the great screen which separated the choir from the church of the laity. It was the feast of Saint Agnes, January twenty-first, and a bitter day when the draught from the empty church blew icy through the lattice-work of the screen. But the frost of the January day was warm compared to the chill which held icebound his frosty, hungry, empty heart.

As he stood there, frozen in body and soul, he was suddenly caught up in rapture, and for the space of an hour and a half tasted joy unspeakable. God himself had taken possession of that human loving heart of his; and in his embrace all wishes were stilled, desire found its fulfilment.

At last he returned to himself in great anguish of body and desolation of spirit; hungering now, not for human companionship, but for the heavenly joys that for so brief a space of time had been his. Leaving the choir, he made his way into the cloister, the same in outward appearance, but inwardly another man. For now his face was not merely turned from evil, it was looking upward, shining in the glow of love and beauty. He passed hither and thither on his various duties, silent and unnoticed, his soul tasting again in memory the bliss of the touch of God. His studies were progressing rapidly, and this progress brought with it a most precious privilege, for he was given a cell to himself instead of studying with the others in a compartment of the common dormitory.

Ever in the depth of his heart rested the memory of the vision he had seen; in his inmost soul he felt time and again the brightness of heavenly glances, and it seemed to him as if he floated on air; the heavenly savour rested with him for a long time afterwards, and this gave him a great and yearning desire for God.

Thus began for Friar Henry a joyous springtide of heavenly romance. The vision in the choir on Saint Agnes's day was only a prelude to other favours. It was in the very hey-day of the age of chivalry and so it seemed fitting to Henry, the Knight of God, that he should seek a Mistress, a fair Bride to whom he might offer his knightly devoirs. He was a lover seeking a love; but God is also the Lover, he empties that he may fill and in many guises he stoops to woo the soul. To Henry the brilliant student, already half in love with knowledge, he came in the guise of divine Wisdom.

The silence of the Dominican refectory is as profound as that of the church and no prior may dispense the brethren. They sit on either side the length of the room, on forms or stools placed along the walls on one side of the long tables which are raised on low platforms. At the top, under the crucifix, sits the prior and with him any honoured guests. Two servers pass the dishes—first the principal dish and then the pittance—offering these dishes first to those of lower rank and ending with the superiors as the angels did in the days of Saint Dominic; while from the pulpit the reader ministers at the same time to the spiritual nourishment of the brethren. It was here that Henry first saw the beauty of the countenance of divine Wisdom.

He was seated at dinner one day when suddenly the words of the reader struck with irresistible force on mind and heart. He was reading from the Book of Proverbs:

My son, hear the instruction of thy father and forsake not the law of thy mother.

If wisdom shall enter into thy heart and knowledge please thy soul, counsel shall keep thee and prudence preserve thee.

For they that are upright shall dwell in the earth and the simple shall continue in it.

She is more precious than all riches; and all things that are to be desired are not to be compared with her. Length of days is in her right hand; and in her left hand riches and glory.

Her ways are beautiful and all her paths peaceable.

The beginning of wisdom get wisdom; and with all thy possessions purchase prudence.

Take hold of her and she shall exalt thee; thou shalt be glorified by her when thou shalt embrace her. She shall give to thy head increase of graces and protect thee with a noble crown.

And as he listened to these words, Henry felt his whole soul drawn to espouse the gracious lady Wisdom as his bride; and considering the matter he thought within himself:

"If she could only be mine, then I should be rich indeed." But as he rested in the joy of this desire, another thought followed which struck a chill of fear. "Shall I love that which I have never seen? I do not even know what Wisdom is. We all know that a handful of our own is better than a houseful in prospect. They who raise lofty buildings and live venturesomely have but a hungry time of it."

As he was considering the matter under this new aspect, thinking within himself how unending is the pursuit of Wisdom, and how hard is the life of the man who follows her, swift as an arrow an inspiration from God pierced his heart: "By ancient right, love and suffering go together. There is no lover but he is a sufferer; no wooer but he is a martyr. Therefore it is not unjust that he who aims so high in love should meet with some things from which he shrinks." And with this thought he was for a time comforted.

But, as in early springtide days of bright sunshine and bird songs alternate with days when cold winds sweep raw over the countryside and night frosts nip the tender buds, so in this early spring of Henry's love there were chill times, and temptations to seek for the sensible warmth of earthly loves would grip him. But he soon learnt that it had now become impossible for him to give himself unreservedly to any creature; the void in his nature was filled; and though sensible spiritual love had not yet given place to the naked love of Christ crucified, the winter of his loneliness was past and gone.

CHAPTER III

THE NAME

IT was full springtide in the soul of Henry Suso. All exterior events passed unheeded, for the glow of love in his soul absorbed also his sensitive faculties, and his whole life, both spiritual and artistic, was caught up in one May song which coloured everything with its brightness. Those of us who live in temperate, sea-washed lands have no conception of the glory of spring after an icebound winter. Suso's mind and heart had been an icy steppe, hard, dry and swept by cold winds; suddenly, "the winter is now past, the rain is over and gone. The flowers have appeared in our land; the time of pruning is come; the voice of the turtle is heard in our land. The fig tree hath put forth her green figs; the vines in flower yield their sweet smell." And so he was forever seeking new ways in which to express the pent-up joy of his soul.

This man who has been called the " Minnesinger in prose and in the spiritual order" took his daily life as he and the others in the priory were living it, touched it with all the glow and romance of his age, and so made it into one lovely song. He was seated at table one day when he heard these words read:

I was exalted like a palm tree in Cades, and as a rose plant in Jericho. As a fair olive tree in the plains, and as a plane tree by the water, in the streets was I exalted. I gave a sweet smell like aromatical balm and cinnamon; I yielded a sweet odour like the best myrrh.

And he wondered within himself who this Beloved of his might really be. Was the loved one God or humankind? Man or woman?

And whilst he was turning this over in his mind, Wisdom

showed herself to him, floating high above him in a choir of clouds; shining like the morning star in radiance; dazzling as the sun. Her crown was eternity; her vesture bliss; her words sweetness; her embrace the fullness of delight. She was far yet near; high yet lowly; present yet hidden. At one moment he thought he saw in her a beautiful maiden, and straightway he saw her as a noble youth. Sometimes she showed herself to him as one rich in wisdom, at other times as overflowing with love. She drew near to him, greeted him smiling and sweetly said: "My son, give me thy heart!"

Then, turning mind and heart inward to gaze on his loveliest Love, he whispered within himself: "I loved her above health and beauty, and chose her instead of light; for her light cannot be put out."

All those whom God calls to his close service must go out into the desert, but for the most part he leads them out by pleasant paths; and so the soul of Henry, in this its spring-time, was fired with such an intense flame of divine love, that he was for ever seeking fresh fuel to feed the flame.

It happened one day when this pain was almost unbearable that he went to his cell to be alone. And as he knelt in prayer, the desire of his soul to possess some token that he might bear on his body as a sign of the interchange of love between him and his divine lover grew so intolerable that he cried aloud:

"Sweet Lord! If only I could find some love token which might be an everlasting sign of love between me and thee; a sign that I am thy beloved, and that thou art the only beloved of my heart; a sign which no forgetfulness of mine shall ever be able to blot out."

Then the thought came to him that to carry the holy name of Jesus over his heart would give him the love token he was seeking; for, in that way, the adorable name would always be present with him to his life's end. So, taking a sharp style, he called on God to help him, saying:

"Mighty God give me strength and power to carry out my desire, for thou must be burnt into my inmost heart."

Then thrusting the style in and out of the bare flesh over his heart, he wrote in letters of blood the sacred name JESUS.

When he had finished, he left his cell to go to the church and kneeling before the crucifix which hung over the pulpit, all bloodstained as he was, he prayed these words:

"Lord, I cannot myself imprint thee more deeply on my heart; but do thou complete the work and imprint thyself deep down in my inmost soul, and so inscribe thy sacred name, that thou mayst never depart from me."

His heart's love heard his prayer; for when the wounds that he had made were all healed, still the sacred name remained there, above his heart in letters the thickness of a cornstalk, in length that of the joint of his little finger, to throb in love with every heartbeat.

Matins ended, Henry was accustomed to go to his cell, and there to rest a little seated on a wooden bench. As the watchman of the city made his first morning round, crying out that it was now daybreak, and that the morning was wet or fair as the case might be, Henry would fall on his knees to salute Mary, Queen of Heaven, as the Daystar. After he had done this he would prostrate in *venia*,[1] offering his morning greeting to his beloved Spouse the Eternal Wisdom, saying: "My soul hath desired thee." His third salutation was to the highest of the seraphim, that one who flames upward in hottest and most fiery love; and at the same time he would beg the Spirit of Love to inflame his own heart with burning love of the Eternal Wisdom, that he might be both on fire himself, and also strong to kindle the hearts of all men by his love and teaching. After that he would go to say prime in choir.

If a new piece of clothing were given him, he used to ask our Lord, who had bestowed it on him, to wish him joy in

[1] The *venia* is a particular form of prostration used by Dominicans.

the wearing of it. He would also beg the giver to allow him to wear it in fulfilling his all-lovely will.

When he went to the refectory, he used to kneel in spirit before the Eternal Wisdom saying:

" My Lord, with the longing desire of my heart I invite thee to go with me, and I pray thee, as thou dost bountifully feed me, to be with me, granting me thy gentle presence at my meal."

Then sitting down, in spirit he would place opposite to him the dear Guest of pure souls; and he would look at him very lovingly, often bowing to him as he pictured him at his side. As he received his portions of food, he used to lift the platter to his divine host—for in a religious house our Lord is the master, and the religious the guests—asking him to bless it. Sometimes he would say:

"O my God, bless what is before us, and vouchsafe to eat with thy servant." Before he drank, he used to lift the goblet and ask our Lord to drink first. He always drank five times; once from each of the wounds of his divine Lord. He ate the first and last morsel of his food in union with the love of the Sacred Heart. If he had before him a portion of food which he found unpalatable, before eating it he used to dip it into the wounded heart of his Beloved; knowing that to do this was to turn all that is hard and bitter into something sweet and delightful.

The feasts of the Liturgy gave Friar Henry opportunity to surround his Beloved with all the delicate attentions his loving heart could devise.

In that part of Swabia where he was born, it was the custom for young men to go out on New Year's eve to beg for May wreaths, as they called it; that is, they would serenade their sweethearts with improvised songs and verses, in return for which the maidens would give them garlands of flowers.

On New Year's eve the memory of this custom flashed through Henry's mind; he pictured what he had so often heard and seen, the flashing of lanterns over the snow, the bursts of light laughter, the snatches of song. Into his heart came the thought that he also would go that night to beg a May wreath from his Love, the Eternal Wisdom.

Accordingly, before the break of day, he slipped to the far end of the dormitory where the statue of our Lady always stands. And there, before the image of the Mother holding in her arms her little Son, the Eternal Wisdom, he began with sweet voiceless melody to sing a sequence in her honour. Was his song perhaps the *Inviolata*?

> O Mary, thou art inviolate, untouched, and chaste,
> Thou hast been made the shining Gate of Heaven.
> O kind, O most beloved Mother of Christ,
> Receive the loving homage of our praise.
> That we may be pure in mind and body
> Thee we importune with desire and with word.
> By the sweet sound of thy intercession
> Obtain eternal pardon for us,
> Most gracious one, who alone remainest inviolate.

There he knelt, asking the Mother's leave to petition for a May garland from her Son; and begging of her that, should his unworthy prayer be unheard, she herself would help him to obtain his desire. Then when his song to the Mother was ended, he turned to his heart's love, the Eternal Wisdom, bowed down in spirit at his feet, he praised him in words and songs, in thoughts and desires as best he could. At last his voiceless praise broke into words:

Thou, my Beloved, art an Easter Day of joy to me.
Thou art the bliss of summer to my heart,
And the hour of my delight.
Thou art the Loved One, whom alone my wayward heart
Loves and thinks on, scorning all earthly love.
Let this avail me now, my heart's Beloved,
And let it gain a wreath from thee this day.
Ah! dearest Lord, for thy almighty power's sake,
And for thine innate goodness infinite,
Let me not go from thee with empty hands this New Year's eve.

18

Such mercy well beseems thee, sweetest Love.
Remember what thy servant Paul has said of thee,
That in thee is not "Yea" and "Nay" but only "Yea" and
  "Yea."
Therefore, my heart's Beloved, say to me this day
A loving "Yea" in answer to my prayer;
And as the foolish lovers of this world
Receive an earthly garland from their fickle loves,
So let my longing soul receive as New Year's gift
Some special Grace, some light from thy fair hand,
My own sweet Love, Wisdom Divine.

And he never left the altar with his prayer ungranted.

For three days before Candlemas he was accustomed to
prepare a spiritual triple candle. The first branch was in
honour of our Lady's virginal and stainless purity; the
second in honour of her unfathomable humility; the third
in honour of her maternal dignity. He prepared this candle
by the daily recital of three *Magnificats*.

When the day itself dawned, he was the first in church,
watching for the Virgin Mother and her little Son. When
she came to the outer gate of the city, he ran to meet her
with the multitudes of souls who love God, and hastening in
front of her, he begged her to pause for a moment while he
sang something in her honour. So with voiceless, spiritual
melody, he sang the *Inviolata,* praying her to show her kindness to a poor sinner. Then with his lips still moving in
soundless song, he rose and followed her with his spiritual
candle, praying that she would never permit the burning
flame of divine light and love to be extinguished in his
heart. Joining the whole multitude of loving souls he began
to sing:

Adorn thy bridal chamber, O Sion,
And receive there Christ the King.
Embrace the Gate of Heaven, Mary chaste,
For she it is who bears the King of Glory.
This Virgin bears within her a new Light
Carrying in her arms her little Son
Begotten eternally before the Morning Star,

When Simeon receiving in his arms,
Proclaimed him to the peoples Lord of Life and Death,
And Saviour of the world.

And thus, with songs of praise, he led them as far as the temple. After this, drawing near to our Lady before she entered and gave the Child to Simeon, he knelt before her, prayed her to show him her Son, and to permit him to kiss him. She offered the Child to him, and spiritually he received and embraced his Beloved; contemplating the beautiful eyes, looking on the little hands, and kissing the tender mouth. Then in his heart he uttered a cry of amazement, to think that he who bears up the heavens is so great and yet so small; so beautiful in heaven, so childlike on earth. At last, giving the Child back to his Mother, he entered the temple with her and remained there until all things were accomplished.

At the time of the Carnival, when for the three days preceding Lent all the world went mad, Henry kept a spiritual carnival in his heart. First, he considered the shortness of the earthly carnival, and that for a momentary joy men purchase for themselves an eternity of suffering. Then he said a *Miserere* in reparation for all the sins and dishonour offered to God. Next he considered that carnival which is a prelude to eternity, of how God makes merry with his friends while they are still clothed in this mortal body; and then, full of joy in God, he recalled all the gifts and blessings he himself had received.

When the month of May came round, on the eve of May the first, the friar was accustomed to set up a spiritual May bough, and to honour it every day for a long space of time. Considering which was the most beautiful of all the trees that grew, he could think of none so fitted to be a May bough as the tree of the Holy Cross whose finding is commemorated on May the third. For that tree blooms more exquisitely with graces, virtues, and other spiritual flowers than any other tree that has ever blossomed. Under this

May bough he made six *venias*, and at each prostration he desired in his contemplation to adorn this tree of life with all the loveliest things which May brings forth. And in his heart he sang his own version of *Salve Crux*:

Hail, holy May bough, tree of wisdom infinite,
Tree on which hung ruddy fruit, prize of everlasting bliss.
First I offer thee this day, roses red of fiery love,
Lowliness for violet, lilies of a pure embrace.
Here for flowers of heath or down, forest, plain, or leafy tree,
Meadows starred with brilliant bloom, a kiss from loving, yearning heart.
Now, for songs of blithesome birds, singing on their Mayday flight,
Hear the song my soul intones, loving praises without end.
Last, for every May bough gift, thee I magnify in song.
Grant that this my earthly praise may bring forth everlasting fruit.

Sometimes the angels sang and danced with him. Once, before daybreak on their festival day, an angel appeared to him in the guise of a heavenly musician, accompanied by many others. The leader, who seemed to be a prince angel, came up to the friar and told him that God had sent them to comfort him and that he must dance and sing with them. So joyous was the measure and melody that, when they began to dance and sing, Henry was drawn in to dance with them. This is what they sang:

PUER NATUS EST NOBIS

A Child is born in Bethlehem, Alleluia.
Whence joyeth all Jerusalem. Alleluia, Alleluia.
  Our joyous hearts his throne,
    The Babe anointed we adore
  With song as yet unknown.

He lieth in the manger poor, Alleluia.
Whose reign for ever will endure. Alleluia, Alleluia.
  Our joyous hearts his throne,
    The Babe anointed we adore
  With song as yet unknown.

21

The ox and ass see in the stall, Alleluia.
The Child who is the Lord of all. Alleluia, Alleluia.
   Our joyous hearts his throne,
     The Babe anointed we adore
   With song as yet unknown.

Kings of Saba from afar, Alleluia.
Offer incense, gold and myrrh. Alleluia, Alleluia.
   Our joyous hearts his throne,
     The Babe anointed we adore
   With song as yet unknown.

We praise one God in Persons Three, Alleluia.
Thanks be to Holy Trinity. Alleluia, Alleluia.
   Our joyous hearts his throne,
     The Babe anointed we adore
   With song as yet unknown.

And the dance, like the heavenly melody, was quite unlike any earthly measure; being, as it were, a swelling up and then falling back again into the wild abyss of God's hiddenness. Presently the angels disappeared, leaving the friar with a deep sense of joy which remained long.

Of course Henry was an enigma to the rest of the brethren. They knew him to be a brilliant scholar, but outside his study he seemed to live in a world of his own. When they spoke to him there was always such a long pause before he answered. At first they used to wonder what was at the back of it all; later they ceased to give the matter much thought. After all, he was odd, and that was an end of it.

"He is quite ignorant of earthly things," said they, "for he does nothing but gape continually to heaven."

Henry was supremely unconscious of the effect of his life on others, for he was living in a world entirely his own, blissfully happy and utterly unaware of what was going on around him. But such a life is not sanctity, it is hardly the prelude to sanctity. True sanctity consists in union with God by faith. A strong, forceful, sensitive nature had been taken captive by divine love; but though the current of its desire had been changed, the soul had not yet been tamed.

It was only through the dark road of our Saviour's Passion that Henry Suso was to attain to true love of God.

CHAPTER IV

THE CALL

In order to understand the next phase in Henry Suso's life, it is absolutely necessary to bear in mind the century in which he lived. Side by side with the entire lack of many things which we regard as simple necessaries, there was much semi-barbaric profusion and luxury. Though windows were for the most part unglazed and there were but few chimneys to be seen even in the great cities, though sanitation was primitive and the streets were foul, yet gold and silver plate were in common use even among the burghers, the streets were gay with folk in silks, satins and furs. Not fifty years previously, following the fashion of the Emperor, the nobles had lived like eastern princes.

It was also a lawless age. The cities were fighting for freedom from the control of the feudal lords who owned the land; the hardy men of the Swiss cantons were fighting for autonomy; the State was fighting for independence in temporal matters from the jurisdiction of the Church; and the Emperor was fighting the Pope. The men of the fourteenth century were a strong, virile race, full of energy both for good and for evil, with passionate natures which required heroic methods to their taming. There was much vice of an open, gross kind, such as modern fastidiousness turns from in disgust; and yet, before God, it is more pardonable than the scientific, unnatural vices of an age when men's bodies have grown soft in luxury and decadence.

The good people of Henry Suso's time punished their

bodies in a way that makes us shudder. Perhaps now, in this pampered age, salvation for many a nation may lie in the cold, the desolation, the hunger and the ruin of bombed cities. In very truth, Almighty God has himself imposed the vigils—cold, fasting and physical pain of which men have grown afraid.

There are three good reasons for penance; namely, expiation for personal sin, expiation for the sins of the world, and the imperious call of love to follow the Beloved and to become like to him. The soul which is carried out of itself by love of a crucified Spouse must of necessity become crucified likewise.

In answer to the question which naturally arises: Why Henry Suso and not I? the answer comes from our Lord: "All men take not this word but they to whom it is given." We can only pursue the path of corporal mortification in so far as we receive a personal, imperative and unmistakable call. This call came to Friar Henry.

For a long time after his first conversion he had been treated as a child, led by God along the path of sweetness, his soul filled with consolations. And so happy was he in his spiritual life that in his contemplation he eagerly sought all subjects which had reference to the Divine nature. The sufferings of our Lord on which he ought to have meditated seemed to him hard and bitter. His pleasure-loving nature, which rejoiced in beauty, shrinking from pain, had turned from the gratification of the senses, to find its delight in spiritual joys, which in their own way also touched the senses, and for this reason he shrank from contemplation of the Passion. Our Lord rebuked him for this, saying:

"Knowest thou that I am the door through which all true friends of God must pass if they would reach true happiness? Thou must tread the path of my suffering humanity, if thou wouldst verily and in deed arrive at my naked Divinity."

Poor Friar Henry! He was still very much of a child, for

he was filled with consternation when he thought of forsaking the pleasant path of spiritual joy and treading the barren road of suffering. It cost him a great effort; nevertheless, in obedience to our Lord's command, he began to meditate on the Passion, though to do so went sorely against the grain. But after he had given himself in earnest for some time to the study of our Lord's sufferings, he found that he began to understand many things of which he had before been entirely ignorant; and so, being a good student, he set himself wholeheartedly to practise what he had learnt.

It had been his custom, as we have seen, when matins was ended, to go to his cell for a little rest, sitting on his wooden bench. Now, instead, he went to the chapter-room, that there alone, before the altar, he might unite himself in spirit with the sufferings of Christ, his Lord and King.

One of the smaller trials of religious life is the difficulty of overcoming a tendency to sleep at the wrong time. When it comes to a pitched battle between the human will and somnolence, he who attempts to remain in one position is lost. To add to Henry's difficulties, he had for so long been accustomed to sleep seated on a hard bench that for him to sit or kneel in the stalls simply invited drowsiness. It was not long before he gave up both these postures and stood up, moving from one corner of the chapter-room to the other so that in this way he might retain during the whole of his prayer a keen sensitiveness to the sufferings of our Lord.

He began his prayer at the altar, then, moving about the room, he followed our Lord on his sorrowful journey until he brought him to Pilate. He did not go into the judgement hall, but waited humbly outside until his Master had been sentenced to death, and then he followed him on the way of the Cross until Calvary was reached. The *Via Dolorosa* began when Henry knelt at the entrance to the chapter-room and kissed the print of his Lord's foot as he passed out from the praetorium.

Rising, the friar made his way into the cloister, and then,

guiding himself by one hand on the stone wall, he repeated the XXI Psalm:

O God, my God, look upon me, why hast Thou forsaken me?
Far from my salvation are the words of my sins . . .
But I am a worm and no man; the reproach of men and the outcast of the people.
All they that saw me have laughed me to scorn,
They have spoken with the lips and wagged the head . . .
Depart from me; for tribulation is very near;
For there is none to help me.
Save me from the lion's mouth, and my lowness from the horns of unicorns.

The four cloisters were four streets down which he followed his Lord. As he went down the first he prayed for grace to leave friends and all temporal goods, that he might follow Christ in desolation and voluntary poverty. On reaching the second cloister he trod under foot all worldly honours and dignities, for the sake of him who was "a worm and no man, and an outcast of the people." When he kissed the ground at the entrance to the third cloister he gladly laid at our Saviour's feet all thought for the needs and comfort of his body, in honour of our Lord's pain and weakness as the soldiers drove him pitilessly on.

At the fourth cloister he pictured our Saviour's coming to the city walls—for he was crucified without the gate—and he knelt in spirit at the gateway through which he must pass. Then falling on his knees, he kissed the ground and prayed his Lord not to go to death alone, but to permit his servant to go with him. As with the eye of his heart he saw our Lord passing quite close to him, he cried out:

"Hail, my Lord and my King! Hail, Son of David! Blessed is he who cometh in the name of the Lord. Hosanna in the highest!"

The Cross followed, resting on our Lord's shoulders, and carried from behind by Simon of Cyrene, and Henry cried out: "Hail, O Cross! Our only hope." Then he rose and watched it go past him.

He knelt again as he saw John pass leading our Lady, Heaven's Queen. As he marked her tears and the unfathomable anguish of her soul, he cried out to her: "Hail, Holy Queen! Mother of Mercy, hail!"

Then he rose and followed our Lord until he caught up with him; and at times the scene he was contemplating was so vivid to his consciousness that he felt as though he were actually bodily present.

When he had reached the summit of the hill, he made an offering of his own will in absolute conformity with the will of God, desiring only that God should use him as he would. He repeated the prophecy:

Who hath believed our report, and to whom is the arm of the Lord revealed? He shall grow up as a tender plant before him, and as a root out of the thirsty ground. There is no beauty in him nor comeliness; and we have seen him and there is no sightliness in him that we should be desirous of him. . . . Despised and the most abject of men, a man of sorrows and acquainted with infirmity; and his look is as it were hidden and despised. Whereupon we esteemed him not. . . . Surely he hath borne our infirmities and carried our sorrows; and we have thought of him as it were a leper, and as one struck by God and afflicted. . . . But he was wounded for our iniquities; he was bruised for our sins. The chastisement of our peace is upon him; and by his bruises we were healed.

As he prayed thus, he went in by the door of the choir and mounting the pulpit steps, he knelt before the crucifix, and there he begged our Lord to grant that neither life nor death, neither joy nor sorrow, should separate him from the love of his heart. Then he would slip up to his cell in the darkness, so that no brother coming down early to prime should find him keeping vigil.

Henry made another Way of the Cross, and that was during the procession which Dominicans make to the Lady altar after compline singing the *Salve Regina*. In spirit he saw the Mother of God standing by her Son's grave, bowed down with all a mother's grief; and he knew that it was time for him to lead her home.

As soon as the *Salve* began he prostrated in spirit at the sepulchre, then bowing down before her, he supported her in the arms of his soul, sharing her grief and trying to comfort her by the thought that, on account of this suffering, she was now a Queen in dignity; our life, our sweetness and our hope. He brought her to the gate of the city and looked back on her, forsaken and with none to comfort her.

At the words "Turn then, most gracious Advocate," he received her with another *venia*, telling her to be comforted since she was the worthy advocate of all. He begged her, by that love which shone forth in the midst of her anguish, to turn her merciful eyes on him and, when he stood before the gate of death, to show him her Son, the fruit of her august womb.

He made the third *venia* before the door of Saint Anne's house and, as he did so, he commended himself to her gentleness and lovingkindness by the words: "O clement, O loving, O sweet Virgin Mary." And he prayed her to receive his soul in its last passage, to be its guide and defence from its worst enemies, leading it to everlasting bliss in Paradise.

Having learnt the lesson of the Passion, Henry had another terrible struggle to put it into practice. His real love for his crucified Lord called him imperiously to imitate him, but his ease-loving nature held him back, for he hated pain. But the call to do yet more was a real and personal one. Love cannot rest content until the body, stripped of all its passions, no longer holds the soul back in its flight to God. So the Minnesinger of the Crucified made of his body a responsive musical instrument; a lyre on whose strings he played the harmonies of his heavenly songs.

Since there is nothing purely negative in the spiritual life, all cutting off is a pruning undertaken with the purpose of bringing forth flowers and fruit; so Friar Henry chastised his body that his spirit might go free, and in this he was a true son of Saint Dominic. His corporal penances were of two kinds; sometimes he invented ways of making his body suffer; at other times, with the ingenuity of love, he used existing conditions to obtain the sufferings for which he thirsted.

As an example of the last, his night-time penances may be quoted. The Dominican bed was hard, but he made it still harder by sleeping on an old door. The friars slept in their clothes, and it is only within the last hundred years that unpleasant insects have been regarded as other than disagreeable though inevitable bedfellows. Henry fastened his belt round his neck and padlocked his hands into it in such a way that he could not move them to give himself any relief from the pest. He discarded the padlock, only to encase his hands in a pair of gloves studded with nails which tore his flesh every time he tried to obtain ease from the irritation. In addition to this, he made for himself a terrible belt studded with nails which he wore fastened tight round his body. Later he made a cross fitted with thirty long sharp nails. The first time he put this on he found the pain so unendurable that he tore it off and blunted the nails. But he soon grew ashamed of his "unmanly cowardice," and with a file pointed them again. To help him bear the pain he chiselled on the back of the cross the name of Jesus.

He drank only once in the day, and that was at the morning breakfast when he was not yet thirsty. He made a little cup which held just sufficient to moisten his mouth, and except on Easter day the only drink he took was water. In the hot weather he suffered intensely, and once when the pain of his parched mouth had moved him to tears, our Lord appeared to him in vision, saying:

"Mark and see how thirsty I was in my death agony, with nothing but a little vinegar and gall to drink; and yet all the cool fountains on the earth were mine, for I had created them as well as all else. Therefore, if thou wouldst

29

imitate me thou must also patiently endure privation and want."

Friar Henry was very finely and sensitively made, he was very human, and still in many ways imperfect, so that the harmonies he played were sometimes gay and joyful, and sometimes in a plaintive minor. He had not yet learnt the perfect art of the minnesinger, the gay and joyful songs of the troubadour.

Sometimes he was filled with joy at being able to offer the praise of sacrifice to his Beloved, and as he sat at supper hungry and thirsty he would say to our Lord:

"Heavenly Father, receive this cool drink of my thirst as an offering of my heart's blood, and give thy Only-Begotten Son to drink of it in that thirst wherewith he thirsted in his death agony on the Cross."

But at other times, standing by the fountain in the cloister, sheer physical desire would overcome all spiritual delight in his offering, and he would murmur to himself:

"How hidden, O Lord, are thy judgements! The broad lake of Constance is so near, and the clear Rhine flows all round me, and yet a single drop of water is too dear for me to purchase." But he never yielded, and more than once our Lady, or the child Jesus, appeared to him in vision and gave him drink.

During the twenty-two years that Henry followed this life of mingled joy and suffering, sixteen were spent at the priory at Constance. During that time he finished his course of philosophy and took his lectorship in theology. For the whole of this time he had lived very much alone. There does not appear to have been anyone there who was capable of understanding him. Perhaps he did not wish to have friends and shrank from contact with others; for the deeps of the spiritual life are found in very secret places, and he may have feared to risk losing the joy of his pain even by contact with others. Besides, he was not yet perfect in self-abnegation. Notwithstanding all his exterior penances, he still found pride and self-love rise in rebellion when he had to put up with contradictions from others. What he laid on himself he could endure, but he still shrank from sufferings which came to him but which were none of his seeking. The sight of uncongenial people made him shrink into himself, and he fled from humiliation. He rejoiced in praise, he tells us, and avoided blame.

From the merely human angle, too, his genius was still held locked within him. Several years had yet to elapse before he was able to loose the pent-up stream in the *Little Book of Divine Wisdom*; and a genius held in bonds is a cause of real suffering both to himself and to others.

As the sixteen years drew to their close, Henry began to suffer acutely from temptations, some very real, and some almost quaintly the outcome of his own supersensitive nature. He was lonely again and greatly in need of help from some sympathetic and experienced master in the spiritual life.

It was then that a second beautiful thing happened to him. His provincial decided that this brilliant young man must have further opportunities, so he sent Henry to study for his doctor's degree at the *Studium Generale* at Cologne. And the professor at that time in charge of the school was Master Eckhart.

CHAPTER V

THE MASTER

IT was probably in the summer of 1324 that Henry and a companion set out for Cologne. Henry had already taken his first examination and was to teach as lector while studying for his doctor's degree.

Since the priory at Constance stands on a small peninsula which juts out into the lake just where the Rhine leaves it, it is more than likely that they made at least part of the journey by boat. The course of the Rhine is one of the beauty-spots of Europe, and the two friars travelled past wooded slopes and rich grain and vine lands. Castles like watch-towers frowned from hill-crests, or from the rocky islets which dotted the river.

Sometimes the boatmen used oars, or rigged up a single sail. Sometimes they would be towed by horses, belonging to the baron whose lands happened to abut the river-bank; and for this the merchant would pay toll. When for a time they left the river to travel by land, they went afoot unless some charitable carter gave them a lift. At night, if chance led them to a town where there was a priory of their own or another Order they would spend the night there; otherwise they stopped at the town or village houses of the lord of the manor, when he had hung his shield over the door in sign that wayfarers might seek hospitality—a custom perpetuated in the signboards of inns.

For the most part, Henry was a silent companion, silent and heavy-hearted; for difficulties and temptations of long standing weighed him down, and so far he had met with no one to whom he could open his heart. For nearly nine years he had suffered continual temptations against faith. Ever since he had studied theology, such questions as how was it possible for God to become man tormented him incessantly, and the more he thought the more perplexed he became. He knew that learning is no help, and that such temptations yield only to humble prayer and a firm adherence of will to God; and so he continuously cried to him "with a strong cry and tears," setting his will to endure in patience until it should please his Master to deliver him.

For several years he had been a prey to interior sadness. His first turning to God had been so sudden and swift that his bodily powers had suffered in consequence, and a weak, ailing body weighs down the spirit and doubles the burden of any load.

The worst trial of all, however, would hardly have been possible to another type of mind. The poor poet, having as yet found no outlet for his genius, was tuned too high. He was suffering from terrible temptations to despair, and the prime cause of this was in itself so small that it would have disturbed no other kind of temperament. When he had entered the Order his father, a wealthy man, had made some small transference of property to the friars at Constance. One of his companions, whether from jealousy or from sheer stupidity, was accustomed to tease his fellow novice, telling him that the whole business smacked of simony.

The joker soon forgot the affair; not so Henry, who proceeded to torture himself, brooding over it until it seemed to him that his entire entrance into the Order had been involved in sin, and that therefore there could be no blessing of any kind on his religious life. For years he looked on himself as one of the damned, suffering in consequence the very pains of hell. In recalling the prayer and penance which had been his daily bread throughout these years fresh opportunities are given of realising the generosity and utter self-forgetfulness of his love of God. It was almost impossible for him to find any relief, since such scruples are very difficult to put into words.

When Henry at last reached Cologne he was placed as lector under the special care of Master Eckhart, the regent of studies. Almost immediately the young man found that God had sent him a father and a friend such as is met with not more than twice or thrice in a lifetime; and Eckhart found in his new cursor one after his own heart.

Born at Hackheim in 1260, while still young John Eckhart had entered the Order of Friars Preachers. In 1300 he was lecturing at Paris, and in 1302 he took his doctorate. After an interval during which he was Provincial of Saxony, in 1311 he was again lecturing at Paris. In 1314 he was teaching at Strassburg, and in 1320 was appointed the first master of the newly erected *Studium Generale* at Cologne.

A profound mystic and at the same time an able man of affairs, he showed himself a true Dominican by uniting contemplation to great activity. One of his lectors was Nicholas of Strassburg, another mystic, who had also been educated at Paris. And studying under these with Suso was the "admirable Tauler."

While Friar Nicholas was teaching the importance of good works, penance and the sacraments, for only through these means can there be perfect conversion of heart and true love of God, Eckhart was lecturing on the divine essence, the relation between God and man, and the return of all created things to God. This man, who has been called the Father of German mysticism, was a follower of Saint Thomas Aquinas and Saint Albert the Great, though in his lectures he departed from the scholastic form. He gave Suso and Tauler his ideas and a clear simple style of expression.

It was not long before Henry opened his whole heart to the master, and in the wisdom and lovingkindness of the other he found peace. Under his direction Suso began to write; for during this period at Cologne he wrote a mystical work entitled *Buchlein der Wahrheit*. Possibly it was the thesis that he prepared for his doctorate, for it is a theologian's book written for theologians.

Eckhart taught Suso not only by word but by example, for the year after the latter went to Cologne the master fell under a cloud. A charge had been carried to Pope John XXII that the German friars were disseminating false doctrine, and Eckhart's name was among those accused. In point of fact, when preaching he occasionally let fall expressions which could be interpreted in a Quietist sense; though other words used in the same sermon usually corrected the false impression which might have been given. Nicholas of Strassburg was appointed Visitator General of the Province by the Pope and he instituted an inquiry. He examined Eckhart's doctrine and writings and declaring them orthodox, closed the process.

In 1327 Heinrich, Archbishop of Cologne, started an independent inquiry into this same matter of Eckhart's orthodoxy, reversed the decision of Nicholas, and arraigned the latter as patron of Eckhart's errors. Both friars appealed to Rome. But within a month, Eckhart had from the Dominican pulpit repudiated any unorthodox sense in which his utterances could be interpreted, retracted all possible errors and submitted in all things to the judgement of the Holy See.

In this same year Suso was to have taken his doctor's degree, but he was warned in a vision that this was not God's will for him: "Thou knowest well enough how to give thyself to God, and to draw other men to him by thy preaching." So he returned to Constance to teach.

Probably Henry never saw his beloved master in life again; his work for the younger man was done; he had taught him the secret of life in God, he had brought peace to his soul, and he had unlocked for him the gate which until that time had imprisoned the intimate and personal thought, that quintessence of personality, which our Saxon forefathers called the *breost-horde*. Though Henry went lonely without him, it was a loneliness enriched by possession and memories which could never be taken from him.

Eckhart died the same year and after death his soul appeared to the younger friar blissfully clothed in ineffable glory, and quite transformed in God, to tell him that he had reached heaven.

"How," asked Henry, "do those rest in God who desire here below to satisfy the supreme truth by total abandonment of self, and true and perfect confidence in the omnipotent Creator?"

"Such are his well-beloved," answered Eckhart, "and their souls in heaven are delightfully united to God and quite submerged in the divine essence. But as the abyss of the Divinity has neither form, measure, nor limit, no words

35

can describe the happiness of those blessed souls who are, as it were, drowned in God."

"Tell me, at least," said Henry, "in this our pilgrimage, which is the most useful and efficacious spiritual exercise to reach perfection?"

"It is the renunciation of self and of all dominion over earthly things," answered Eckhart. "It is blind trust in God, resting in him alone. It is to receive all from the Creator and not from creatures. It is to be patient and mild with those who pursue us like savage wolves."

Three years after his return to Constance God made known to Henry that it was his will for the friar to leave his excessive penances and return to the normal way of life of the Dominican. He learnt also that what he had already done was no more than a good beginning, and that God himself would mould him to the likeness of his Son.

So a time of joy and peace set in; a time made fruitful by the writing of a book.

CHAPTER VI

THE BOOK

THE year after Suso's return from Constance, and the death of his friend and master, Eckhart, he wrote *Das Buchlein der Ewigen Weisheit—The Little Book of the Eternal Wisdom*.

It is given to many men to write books; to few men, and that only once or twice in a lifetime, is it given to create a book. *The Little Book of Eternal Wisdom* is a creation.

Henry sat in his cell by the unglazed window which looked out over smooth lawns fringed with beeches, willows and poplars, stretching down to the green waters of the lake, amazingly green against the blue of the sky. Slowly and steadily his pen slipped over the parchment as the magic grew under his fingers. Often he would pause to stare with unseeing eyes across the lake to the slopes beyond, golden-yellow with ripening corn, and blue-green with olive trees. Which word of the two, so much alike in sense, gave the exact shade of meaning he wanted to express? Which fitted most harmoniously with the rest? Then on would go the pen, sure and unhurried, unlocking in rhythmic, alliterative lines of German the rich *breost-horde* of his lover's heart.

In the distance a bell would clang; and at the sound, the writer would lay down his pen, to gaze at the sheets before him quite dazed. He would rise, pause for a second to gather his thoughts from the lovely land of ideals where they had been wandering, and then hasten away to prayer or the lecture-hall. So day by day he wrote on and on, driven forward by the force of inspiration, locking away each sheet as he finished it, never looking back.

At last the book was finished, and with a sigh of regret he laid down his pen to fetch the whole manuscript from the place where he kept it. Then slowly, word by word, phrase by phrase, he read it over, correcting, expanding, deleting; for inspiration was still with him. When he felt he could do no more and that the whole was as perfect as he could make it, before he wrote a fair copy he took the opportunity of an unusually long period of leisure to re-read it. Then, inevitably, came heartbreak, for the vision had been so infinitely lovely, and this rendering of his was so utterly poor and inadequate.

Still he could do no more, so with great diffidence he carried it to his prior, who said he had done well. Well? That pitiful, stammering, halting little book of his? Suso was near laughing. He had conceived the glory of a star, and had brought forth the light of a feeble glowworm. Nevertheless he loved this child of his; how could he do otherwise? Neither could he rest content with what he had done. His prior had possession of the *Buchlein*, but for six years he wrote and rewrote, this time in Latin, calling it *Horologium Sapientiae*, a book which is enriched by its finished language, richness of figure, and rhythmic movement; it was *Das Buchlein* grown up. Years later at Ulm he brought out yet another edition, this time in German again.

The Little Book of Eternal Wisdom is a love song, the singlehearted outpouring of the same young love which had necessitated his terrific penances. For the love given to God is in no way different from that which we should give our fellow men. Human love of God at its highest is like the gold which has passed through the crucible; precisely the same metal which has been taken from the womb of earth, but purified from all that lessens perfection, in the furnace of suffering.

These are a few extracts, taken with slight alterations from Raby's translation, which will serve to illustrate the trend of Henry's spirituality at this time, its ecstasy, and its complete sanity. This is his description of how lovely God is:

I may turn myself hither, I may turn myself thither, in me is nothing that can displease; in me is everything that can delight the inmost wishes of the heart and all the desires of the soul. Lo! I am so good and pure that the man who receives in a life-time but one taste of me counts all the pleasures and delights of the world as naught but bitterness; all its possessions and honours as worthless, fit only to be cast away. My beloved ones are encompassed by my love, and are absorbed into the one only thing; a love without images and without spoken words. They are gathered into me, the good from which they flowed. My love is also able to lift the heavy load of sin from penitent souls, to give them a free and gentle heart, and to create in them a clean conscience. Tell me, what has the world to offer which can outweigh in value this one thing? For he who gives his heart wholly to me lives joyfully, dies securely, and receives the Kingdom of Heaven, even here on earth as well as in the world to come.

Now, behold! I have given thee many words, and yet my

beauty is as little touched by them as the sky by thy little finger; for no eye hath ever seen my beauty, nor ear heard it, nor hath the conception of it entered into any human heart.

And this is his soul's answer:

Ah! Thou lovely and delightful Flower of the field. Thou delight of the heart, as thou restest in the embrace of the pure loving soul. How well is this understood by the man who has ever really felt thee; but how strange is it to him who knows thee not, whose mind and heart are still of the earth earthly. . . .

And again:

O gentle Lord! If only my soul were worthy to be called thy lover! If it were possible that all the delights, all the joy and all the love that this world could offer were to be found in one man, how gladly would I renounce him for thy name's sake.

When he tries to speak of that which he saw without image he is driven to have recourse to images; for "eye hath not seen, nor ear heard, neither hath it entered into the heart of man to conceive" the mysteries of God as he reveals them to his saints, and so such a one must needs use symbols to express that which in itself is without symbol.

ETERNAL WISDOM: Thou shouldst wholly lock thyself up in my love-wounded heart, in my open side, there to dwell, there to seek thy resting-place. Then will I wash thee with the waters of life, and deck thee out in purple with my precious Blood; I will join myself to thee, and unite thee eternally with myself.
THE SERVITOR: Lord, there never was any magnet so powerful to attract hard iron to itself, as thy love-filled Passion, thus offered to my soul, is powerful to unite itself to all hearts . . .

Again:

For this reason when our poor souls are in the narrow prison house of the bottomless sorrows of our hearts, and we can neither stir here nor there, there is nothing left for us but to lift up our eyes to thee, O chosen Queen of Heaven. Therefore, thou Mirror in which is reflected the brightness of the Eternal Sun, thou hidden treasure of Infinite Compassion, this day do I, in union with all penitent hearts, salute thee.

In contemplating the Passion, which is the supreme expression of God's love for man, Friar Henry reached a sure foundation-stone on which to build the edifice of his own love of God. As the Eternal Wisdom himself told his servitor:

Behold! assiduous meditation on my Passion makes of a simple man a master of high learning; for truly it is a living book in which everything is to be found. Blessed is the man who has it at all times before his eyes.

And this is how he must study the Book of the Passion:

The contemplation of my sufferings must not be treated cursorily as one may find convenient time and place; but they must be studied in heartfelt love and sorrowful sympathy. . . . If thou hast no taste to contemplate my Passion with weeping eyes, as thou considerest the bitter agony that I suffered, thou oughtest to contemplate it with a laughing heart, because of the joyous profit thou wilt find in it. And if thou hast no mind either to laugh or to cry, thou oughtest to meditate on it in the dryness of thy heart, to my honour and praise. In doing this thou wilt have done no less than if thou hadst really overflowed with tears, and been steeped in sweetness. Since it is then that thou dost act from love of virtue, without regard to thyself.

The soul must give herself to God through self-crucifixion!

Thou shouldst give thyself and all that is thine cheerfully to me and never take it back. Thou shouldst leave untouched all that is not absolutely necessary to thee; then will thy hands be truly nailed to the Cross. Thou shouldst gaily set about doing good works and persevere in them; then will thy left foot be made fast. Thy inconstant mind and wandering thoughts shouldst thou make constant and collected in me, and thus will thy right foot be nailed to the Cross. Thy powers of mind and body must not seek rest in lukewarmness, in the likeness of my arms ought they to be stretched out and distended in my service. In honour of my dislocated bones thy sickly body must often be wearied out in spiritual exercises, and so made incapable of following thy own desires. Many an unknown suffering must strain thee to me on the narrow bed of the Cross, so shalt thou become lovely like me and of the rosy hue of blood. The withering away of thy sensitive nature must make me blooming again; thy hardships willingly borne must be a rest to my weary back; thy resolute resistance to sin must relieve my spirit; thy devout heart must soften my pains, and thy strong flaming heart must kindle my heart.

Here lies the secret of the unalterable serenity with which the friar faces all kinds of suffering and pain:

When thou dost strive to do thy best as well as thou dost understand it, and for so doing dost earn from thy fellow men only scornful words and contemptuous gestures; when they so utterly despise thee in their hearts that they look upon thee as unable, nay afraid, to avenge thyself for injuries, and still thou continuest not only firm and unshaken in thy conduct, but dost lovingly pray for thy revilers to thy heavenly Father, and dost sincerely excuse them before him; lo! as often as thou diest thus to thyself for love of me, so often is my death freshly renewed and made to bloom again in thee. When thou dost keep thyself pure and innocent, and still thy good works are so misrepresented that with the joyful consent of thy heart thou art reckoned among the wicked, and from the bottom of thy heart thou art ready to forgive all the injuries thou hast received at the hands of thy persecutors as though they had never happened, and moreover thou dost assist thy persecutors by word and deed in imitation of my forgiveness of my persecutors; then truly thou art crucified with thy Beloved. . . . Only carry my bitter death in thy heart and in thy prayers and in the manifestations of thy works, then wilt thou fulfil the sufferings and fidelity of my Mother and my beloved Disciple.

He is instructed in the noble game of love:

SERVITOR: When my soul is deserted by thee, she is like a sick person who can relish nothing. . . . I am then drawn to sins, weak in resisting my enemies, cold and lukewarm in everything good. . . . But, Lord, when the bright Morning Star rises in the midst of my soul, all my sorrow passes away, all my darkness is dispelled, and laughing cheerfulness appears. . . . Everything which before was hard and troublesome and impossible becomes easy and pleasant.

ETERNAL WISDOM: Thou art and hast nothing of thyself but imperfection. . . . This is the game of love.

SERVITOR: And what is the game of love?

ETERNAL WISDOM: All the time that Love is with Love, Love does not know how dear Love is. But when Love is separated from Love, then only does Love feel how dear Love is.

SERVITOR: Lord, this is a vexatious game. Alas! Lord, is inconstancy never in any manner laid aside while life endures?

ETERNAL WISDOM: In very few men, for constancy belongs to eternity.

SERVITOR: Lord, who are these men?

ETERNAL WISDOM: The very purest of all, and in eternity most like God.

SERVITOR: Lord, which are they?

ETERNAL WISDOM: Those are the men who have denied themselves in the most perfect manner.

SERVITOR: Lord, teach me what I should do.

ETERNAL WISDOM: Thou oughtest in good days to look to evil ones, and in evil days not to forget good ones; thus neither can elation in my company injure thee, nor can despondency in dereliction. If in thy faintheartedness thou canst not endure my absence with pleasure, at least wait for me in patience and seek me diligently.

Once the friar saw a terrible vision of hell which threw him into a torment of fear lest, when he came to die, he should be separated from his only love, the Eternal Wisdom. Then he was given this simple and consoling answer: "Throw away thy fear; that which is united in time remains undivided in eternity."

It must have been somewhere about this time that our Lord deigned to change Henry's name. Once the divine Wisdom appeared to him and said:

"Henry, fear nothing, for I will be with you. I will help you in all your troubles because I love you in a special way. In proof of my love I will change your name; you will be to me no longer Friar Henry, but Friar Amandus, the lover. If the world is in ignorance of this, the angels in heaven will know it, and one day I will teach it to men likewise, so that all may see how dear my servants are to me."

The humble friar kept the secret of his God-given name until his death. There was only one dear friend to whom, under promise of secrecy, he told it, and this friend kept the secret faithfully as long as the saint was alive.

While Henry was studying at Cologne his mother died, literally of the love of God. One day at the beginning of Lent she went to pray before a carved wooden reredos which hung in the Cathedral at Constance, representing the taking down of our Lord from the Cross. As she knelt there, so great was her sorrow in contemplating the grief of the Mother that at last she fell in a swoon before the altar. Some bystanders lifted her up and carried her home, where she lay sick unto death until Good Friday, when, at the hour of our Lord's death, she died while the Passion was being read to her. Henry knew nothing of her illness until Good Friday night when she appeared to him radiant in glory.

"My son," she said, "love God with all your might, and he will never abandon you in your troubles; it is true that I have left the world, but such a departure is not death, since I am now living happy in heaven, where the divine mercy has rewarded me for the great love I bore to the Passion of Christ."

"My blessed and loving mother," cried the friar, "love me always in heaven as you have done on earth, and never leave me in my troubles."

His father also must have died about this time. He had been a very worldly man, very hard and difficult to live with. He also appeared after death to his son, and told him that, though by the mercy of God and the prayers of his wife and son he had been saved, he was, nevertheless, condemned to suffer very severely in Purgatory. He asked his son to pray for him, told him what were the sins for which he had to make expiation, and instructed him how best to help him reach heaven.

The friar carried out his father's injunctions exactly; and a short time after Count von Berg again appeared to him. This time he was radiant in glory, having been sent by God to thank him for his prayers and penances.

CHAPTER VII

THE POET

AND now, if much of Friar Henry's life is not to remain an enigma, his right to be called a poet must be established; and it is not altogether easy to prove a man a poet when none of his poetry has come down to us! If one asks those who know his life and writing—and to know these is to love the man—the answer invariably is: "Poet? Of course he is a poet." Yet they find it hard to give logical reasons for their belief.

His first claim to be a poet seems the undoubted fact that he was a mystic; for the mystic is God's poet. Such a one is not led by the paths of sense to the obscurity of union with God by faith; rather does the luminous darkness of mystic, infused contemplation pervade even the physical senses. His ecstasies are an overflow of the joys of the soul, an over-whelming flood, poured out from that part of his nature which is above sense; a flood which his senses are not strong enough to withstand.

Just as beauty reacts on the poet's mind and imagination, changing into the rhythmic flow of words, so does the touch of the hand of God on his servants' souls tune even their sensitive faculties to a new and rare perception of beauty, which is again at times translated into winged words. The mystic is God's troubadour, and Henry is known as the "Minnesinger." In an old illuminated manuscript he is represented as holding a lyre, so that in his own times he was reckoned one of the singers. One of the works imputed to him is *Das Minnebuchlein*.

The *Little Book of the Eternal Wisdom* in its medieval German as Suso wrote it is highly alliterative. Even in the English translation there are many traces of "kenning," that is, verses where the second half of the line or phrase is an echo or amplification of the first. Now alliteration and "kenning" were two necessary elements of ancient and medieval poesy and therefore it seems highly probable that the book was originally written in what we now call "free verse." His later work, *Horologium Sapientiae,* is rhythmic, rich in figure and beautiful in diction. He himself constantly refers to the hymns and other verses he was accustomed to compose and recite in his devotions. His Latin prayer in morning salutation to the Eternal Wisdom seems to lend itself to a metrical rendering.

Anima mea desideravit te in nocte,
Sed et spiritu meo in praecordiis meis de mane,
Evigilavi ad te, O praeclarissima Sapientia
Petens ut desiderata praesentia
Tua cunctis nobis adversantia
Penetralia cordis nostri sua multiformi gratia perfundat,
Et in amore tuo vehementer accendat.
Et nunc, dulcissime Jesus Christe,
Ad te diluculo consurgo,
Teque ex intimo cordis affectu saluto.
Milia quoque milium coelestium agminum tibi ministrantium
      Te ex me salutant,
Ac decies millies centena millia tibi assistantium
      Te ex me glorificent,
Universalis etiam harmonia creaturarum
      Te ex me collaudant,
Ac nomen tuum gloriosum protectionis nostrae clipeum benedicant
      In saecula.   Amen.

Since all descriptions of visions are symbolic—a human attempt to express the ineffable—who but a poet could have found a description such as this to symbolise a vision?

It happened once that Henry had been for a long time discoursing on the excellence of divine love. At last, when he was alone, he began to consider of what kind was this Beloved of his, he whom he loved with his whole heart and whose love he preached to others. As he considered, pondering the wonders of Eternal Wisdom, his senses were stilled in ecstasy; and it seemed to him that he was transported to a green and flowering meadow by the side of a young man of heavenly beauty who led him by the hand.

Then the youth began to sing, and the rapture of the song filled the soul of the friar so full of burning love and longing for God that it seemed as if the strength of that love must force his very heart from his breast. When the song was ended he saw before him a picture which was placed there with intent to impress on his mind the words of the song so that he might not forget them.

Looking at the picture, he saw the Mother of God holding her little Son pressed tight to her heart; and above the Child's head were the words of the song exquisitely written, but in such a fashion that only those who had drunk deep of spiritual things could read the words. And the words as Henry read them were these: HEART'S DARLING. Then the Babe looked at the friar with eyes of love and he understood in the depths of his soul the truth that only the divine Babe is our heart's Darling. He took the Babe in the arms of his soul, and pressed him to the very centre of his heart, and began to sing the song he had just learnt. Presently he came to himself and found his hand laid where he had placed it to still the raptures of his heart.

What was this song? He does not tell us. Could it have been the Spring Song that later on he sang to Elsbeth Staglin? I have ventured to give a metrical version; the prose English version will be found in Father Sebastian Bowden's *Life of B. Henry Suso, Written by Himself.*

> Look to the ends of the earth,
> To the height of the sky,
> To the rolling course of the planets,
> To the glittering array
> The lance points of stars in their myriads.

Look to the stars, to the sun,
To the sunshine of spring,
To the leaves and the grass and the flowers
To the birds on the wing,
To the birds and the beasts, winterbound, but free
Now to play,
To love and beget and be joyful.

Look to the sun, to the earth,
To the work of thy power,
O, thou gentlest and greatest,
Creator of fire and flower,
Of air and of river and sea.
Most Beautiful, Maker of beauty,
Of man and of all
That live in ocean and air, that live in thy power.

Thou hast given to great and to small,
To rich and to poor;
Thou greatness of depth beyond depth
Of height beyond height,
O God to adore,
O Lord, our support and delight.

Look to the depths of the sea, the heights of the sky,
To thy Maker and King.
Find him and hold him, rejoice evermore.
See thy God in each creature and thing.
Give thanks and adore.

Who but a poet could have given such a conception to the *Sursum Corda*?

Three thoughts above all move and inflame my heart; sometimes they occur to me in succession, sometimes all together. First, I contemplate in spirit all my being, my soul, my body, all my powers, whether they are in act or merely in capacity to act; and all around me all the creatures with which almighty God has peopled the earth, the heavens and the elements. I contemplate the angels of heaven, the beasts of the forest, the dwellers in the waters, the plants of the earth, the sand of the sea, the tiny motes which float in each ray of sunshine, the snowflakes, the drops of rain, the diamonds of dew. I consider that,

47

even to the farthest ends of creation, every creature obeys God and contributes, in so far as it is able, to the mysterious harmony which ascends without pause to praise and bless the Creator.

I picture myself in the midst of this chorus as choir master, and I apply all my faculties to marking the rhythm correctly; I invite and stir them all by the most lively movements of my own heart, the uplifting of my soul, to sing joyously with me *Sursum Corda. Habemus ad Dominum. Gratias agamus Domino Deo nostro.* Lift up your hearts; we hold them to the Lord; give thanks to the Lord our God.

Next I consider my own heart and those of all men; I think of the joy, the love, the peace of those who dedicate themselves to God alone. Then I call to mind the misfortunes, the tortures, the remorse and the disturbance of those who long for the things of this world with so much solicitude and ardour. Then with all my strength I call on all men who dwell on this earth to lift themselves with me to God, in order to bless and praise him. "O, poor human hearts," I cry, "lift yourselves above the wave which is dragging you to ruin; leave vice and death; break the chains of your hard prison, awake from your sleep of apathy. Let a holy and true conversion lead you to God in order to thank and serve him. *Sursum Corda; Gratias agamus Deo nostro.*"

His interior life seems to have been one great song. Once when he was in his cell praying before the Aurora Mass, resting in peace and stillness of heart, he was suddenly transported to a temple filled with angels and the spirits of the blessed. There surrounding an altar where mass was being celebrated, they were singing: *Sanctus, Sanctus, Sanctus. Benedictus qui venit in nomine Domini.* Their voices were lifted in harmony and Henry sang with them; then it seemed to him that from the Sacred Host there issued a spiritual light which penetrated far into the depths of his heart and soul. It was as though their two hearts—his own and that of his Beloved—were united in an ineffable manner, without intermediary and without any veil or shadow.

Such was Friar Henry, saint and poet; sensitive, highly

strung, with an extraordinary faculty of imagination, and the power of calling up phantasy; exceedingly lovable, and at times exceedingly trying to live with.

I had not long finished this chapter when a friend sent me a leaflet which had been sent to her from Canada ten years ago. She knew nothing about the original of the poem, which was on the reverse side of a page of advertisement. But if it does no more, it at least proves that other folk reckon Suso a poet.

WHAT THOU ART TO ME

Bl. Henry Suso

As the Bridegroom to his chosen,
    As the King unto his realm,
As the keep unto the castle,
    As the pilot of the helm;
So, Lord, art Thou to me.

As the fountain to the garden,
    As the candle in the dark,
As the treasure in the coffer,
    As the manna in the ark,
So, Lord, art Thou to me.

As the ruby in the setting,
    As the honey in the comb,
As the light within the lantern,
    As the mother in the home;
So, Lord, art Thou to me.

As the sunshine in the darkness,
    As the image to the glass,
As the fruit unto the fig-tree,
    As the dew unto the grass;
So, Lord, art Thou to me.

This chapter is fated to receive a series of appendices. After it had been concluded for the first time, a friend sent me the leaflet with the short poem I have given above. After that I made many unavailing attempts to find traces of originals. Then, when all was finished and ready for press, the same friend sent me a book entitled *Hymns of Ter Steegen, Suso and Others* by Frances Bevan, published by James Nisbet, 21 Berners Street, London W.1, 1904. In her preface the author says that she has made this translation for the benefit of the many who are unacquainted with the language of the German authors.

Twelve of these poems are under Suso's name. Some of them are easily recognisable as coming from his autobiography. Therefore, considering also that the autobiography was written for the mystic, Elsbet Stagel, it will hardly be going beyond evidence to conclude that portions of the original were metrical.

CHAPTER VIII

THE RAG

FRIAR HENRY'S purely contemplative life was ended and with it the period of his active purification; his apostolic life was now to begin, bringing with it passive purification. If the first was hard for nature, the second was incomparably harder. This change from contemplative to apostolic life was preceded by a short period during which he rested both body and soul. After twenty-two years during which he had practised every kind of bodily austerity, he had made of his sensitive nature a lyre on which he played the harmonies to accompany his soul's melody of praise. But he had played the lyre himself and this did not carry out to the full the divine purpose. Almighty God was to be the musician and the Minnesinger's mind, body and soul were to be the heavenly psaltery on which he chose to play his Love Song to mankind. And so this instrument must be made absolutely pliant under the divine hand. There was pain before him, it is true, but pain which was to mould his nature to loveliness. This was shown to Henry by means of a symbol.

He was told in vision to open the window of his cell and look out. In the garden below a dog was playing with an old rag that he had found. He was seizing it between his teeth and tossing it in the air; crouching with it between his paws and worrying it; growling as he tore it to pieces. From this the friar understood that God willed him to be as this dog's plaything—the sport and mock of men. For one moment he shrank back appalled; then he said to himself:

"My soul, since it cannot be otherwise, resign thyself to it; and as that rag suffers itself to be maltreated in silence so do thou."

For many years afterwards he kept the torn rag to remind him of this lesson, and when he felt tempted to indulge in self-pity, to which his sensitive temperament made him peculiarly liable, he would take out the rag and look at it, when the memory of the vision restored his peace.

Sometimes also, if he turned away from those who annoyed him with an inward movement of impatience, he would hear a voice within him say: "Remember that I, thy Lord, turned not away my beautiful Face from those who spat on me." And this would make him ashamed of his momentary impatience, and he would turn again very lovingly towards those who had angered him.

So Henry's time of repose was ended; before him lay sufferings, just as sufferings lay behind him. But these new sufferings were of a different type—sufferings in which he was no longer to be his own executioner, but with the full consent of heart and will was to be bound and handed over to others. "Amen, amen, I say to thee, when thou wast younger thou didst gird thyself and didst walk where thou wouldst. But when thou shalt be old, thou shalt stretch forth thy hands and another shall gird thee, and shall lead thee whither thou wouldst not."

How he was to bear himself in patience, passive under the hand of God, was shown to him one day—the feast of Candlemas—when as Henry journeyed to the Temple in spirit with the holy family, the infant Jesus spoke to him:

"Thou dost not yet know how to suffer; but I will teach thee. Behold! When thou art in suffering thou shouldst not look forward to the end of that suffering, fancying that then thou wilt be at rest. But as long as suffering lasts, thou shouldst be prepared to accept with patience the fresh suffering which is sure to follow in its train. Thou shouldst act like a maiden picking roses. When she has picked one rose from the bush this does not satisfy her, but she resolves to pick many more. Even so do thou. Make up thy mind to this beforehand, that when one suffering comes to an end, another will forthwith meet thee."

The spiritual life of the Friar Preacher is neither contemplative nor is it active; it is apostolic. The Preachers' motto: *Contemplata aliis tradere*—to give to others the fruit of contemplation—gives the keynote of the apostolic life. Just as the foundations are dug deeper in proportion to the height of the edifice, so the preacher's apostolate is fruitful only in proportion to the depths of the foundation of his contemplation. For action in the spiritual life must rise out of and be preceded by contemplation. With the Dominican, contemplation implies also active forms of penance; while the second part of the life, *aliis tradere,* implies the passive penance of total submission in all things under the hand of God.

In the treatise called *The Colloquy of the Nine Rocks,* supposed to have been written by Suso much later, in the Lent of 1352, there is a passage which throws high light on the development of the mystic life; and in particular on the mystic life of the Friars Preachers.

Under the symbol of nine rocks, Friar Henry sets out the nine degrees of the spiritual life, in many respects comparable to the mansions of Saint Teresa's *Interior Castle.* The sea which surrounds these rocks is spread with the nets of the devil; and in these nets he entraps sinners and those who do not persevere as dwellers on one or the other of the nine rocks. As, in his vision, Henry is taken from the lower rocks to those higher, he finds their inhabitants more beautiful and shining in the light of grace the higher he goes.

On the ninth rock he finds those who have arrived at the highest degree of perfection; "the hidden children of God and his dearest friends, the true adorers who adore the Father in spirit and in truth." He asks whether these can fall from grace, and he is told that not only is it possible for them to fall, but that such a fall will be like to that of Lucifer who fell through pride. "Because they have not profited by the splendours of divine grace, because they have abused the lights that they received on the rock in order to spread errors and heresies, they become the scourge of the Church, more straitly to be avoided than the demons themselves."

He is then bidden to look in the sea, and among the nets spread by the demon he sees two men; one black as the very devil, the other beautiful and bright as an angel. Of the former he is told that "he was once an inhabitant of the ninth rock; but he began to give way to complaisance in himself and in his knowledge; he sought the company of men in order to show his merit and high virtue, and he fell like Lucifer. He is a captive of the demon and teaches a doctrine full of heresy and error." The other, on the contrary, "is a faithful dweller on the ninth rock. He sees God in his origin and rejoices in his nearness. But, impelled by charity, he has thrown himself among the nets so that he may come near to sinners, in order to help, and if possible convert them. He has placed all his confidence in God and his grace, and as he knows the perils that threaten Christians in the toils of the demon and the awful judgements which, to avenge their ingratitude to God, await them after death, he is full of Christlike pity and would willingly endure in their stead the pains and torments of hell, if by so doing he might deliver them from their sins and the power of the enemy."

Henry then asks if this apostle has nothing to fear from his nearness to sin and sinners, and he is told, "No, because his degree of virtue sets him free from all servile fear. He fears neither persecutions nor torments nor death itself; he has, it is true, a filial fear of not serving God as well as he wishes to, and of failing to imitate the example of Jesus Christ as he desires. He knows God and the joys of heaven in such an ineffable manner that in seeing men deceived by their senses, their flesh and sin, he grieves bitterly over their misfortune and compassionates the sorrows of Mother Church. This is his greatest and heaviest cross; it saps his strength and breaks his heart, and he carries this cross after his Master until death. Only God can comfort him."

This was Friar Henry's vocation, as it is the vocation of all true Friars Preachers, to deliver to others—those in peril, the sinner, those seeking God—the fruits of their own contemplation, trusting in the mercy of him for whose sake they have left the security of the rock to preserve them in the perils they are risking for his sake. In doing the work of God they "become one with him, and who can separate them from him? God will never permit them to fall into the hands of the enemy because they are his close friends, his dearly beloved."

How the friar's active life proceeded from a superabundance of contemplation was shown in a vision to one of his spiritual children. She saw the friar saying mass on a high mountain, while all around him, clinging to him in many different ways, were innumerable children. He was praying for all of them and the closer they clung to him the nearer they were drawn to God. On asking God in her prayer what this might mean, she was told:

"These are his penitents or disciples, or are in other ways bound to him by ties of special love and faithfulness. All these he has commended to me in such sort that I will guide their lives to a good end, and they shall never be parted from my gladsome countenance. Whatever heavy sufferings may befall him on this account, all shall be fully made up to him in the joys that I shall give him."

He had been well prepared for his apostolic life, for, as our Lord told another of his spiritual children:

"I have made his loving heart bright and glorious that the reflection of the radiance streaming forth from his heart may draw the hearts of all men in love of me."

Once, when the friar was in ecstasy, it seemed to him that he was carried to a place where there were a great number of angels, and one of those who was standing by him said: "Put forth thy hand and look at it." Henry did so and, as he watched, from the palm of his hand there sprang out a lovely red rose surrounded with bright green leaves. It was so large that it covered his whole hand, and so bright and beautiful that the sight of it rejoiced his heart. Turning his eyes to his other hand, he saw that another rose was growing from the palm of this also and that there were two more besides, one on either foot. Turning to the angel, he asked:

"Dear comrade, what means this vision?"

"It means sufferings on sufferings, and yet more sufferings, which God wills to give you," answered the angel. "This is the meaning of the four roses on your hands and feet."

"Ah! Gentle Lord," whispered the friar to himself. "It is a strange ordinance of God that suffering should cause such pain to men, and yet, at the same time, make such a lovely spiritual adornment."

For the next ten years or so, Henry experienced sufferings in abundance. Some of his trials were great and heavy, others mere pin-pricks. But who does not know that the big troubles of life are often easier to bear than the countless small rubs of everyday life? Because the first appear to come more directly from God, they are simpler to face than those which come to us from him by way of our neighbour.

A good proportion of Henry's suffering came from his own brethren; which was hard for our saint but, human nature being what it is, quite understandable, for, after all, Henry was unusual. A saint and a mystic is not one of those naturally endowed with the capacity of living unquestioned among others; and should this saint and mystic be also a poet, then he stands out in a way which utterly precludes his being overlooked, however much he himself may desire this.

Towards the end of his life the friar attained such union with God that he sank into the background, but at this time he had not reached the heights of the supremely normal and so he and his brethren often got on each other's nerves. The unusual is very trying to nature when people live day in day out in close contact. Besides Henry's own supersensitive temperament suffered cruelly while other folk could blunt sharpness with a smile and joke. And so these small sufferings were far harder for him to bear than his iron-studded cross, his chain or his discipline. One day, in fact, he grew so heartsick that he went to his cell to complain to God.

"Dear God, Lord of the world, be gentle and gracious to me, a poor man, for I must make my complaint to thee this day. I cannot help it; and though thou owest no man anything, let thy infinite goodness allow a full heart to seek comfort in thee, when it has no one else to tell, or who will comfort it. I call thee to witness, Lord, that all through my life I have had a tender heart. I have never seen anyone sad or suffering without heartfelt pity. I have never willingly listened to talk which would hurt anyone, whether in his presence or absence. All know that I have seldom or never by any words of mine made difficulties for another, either with the prior or anyone else. But I have done my best as far as I could for everyone; and if I could do nothing I was silent, or went away that I might not add to his trouble. I have shown more love for those who were wounded in honour, that they might get back their good name. I am the friend of the poor, and specially of God's friends. All who ever came to me either in sorrow or aggrieved always received good counsel of me so that they went away joyful and consoled; for I wept with those who weep. No one ever caused me any suffering, no matter how great, if he only smiled kindly on me afterwards, in God's name it was all over and past and as if it had never been. O Lord! I will say no more about mankind, for I cannot see or hear of the needs and sorrows of little birds, beasts and other creatures without being grieved to the heart, and praying the kind Lord to help them all. Everything that lives on the earth is treated with favour and kindness by me; and yet, thou, O kind Lord, sufferest some of those of whom Saint Paul speaks, calling them false brethren, to behave exceedingly cruelly to me, as thou well knowest, and as is manifest to all. Alas! kind Lord, look at this and console me with thyself."

After he had opened his heart to God in this way, there came on him a quietness and stillness, and in his ecstasy God spoke to him thus:

"The childish account into which thou hast entered with me comes from this, that thou dost not always keep before thee the words and ways of the suffering Christ. Thou must know that God is not satisfied with mere kindness of heart such as thou professest; he wants still more from thee. What he wants is this, that when thou art openly ill-treated by anyone in words or behaviour, thou shalt not only bear it patiently, but thou shalt die to thyself so utterly as not to go to sleep at night until thou hast sought out thy tormentor and, as far as possible, calmed his angry heart with thy sweet words and ways; for with such meek lowliness thou wilt take from him his sword and knife, and make him powerless in his ill-will. See, this is the old perfect way which the dear

Christ taught his disciples when he said: 'Behold I send you as lambs among wolves.'"

When Henry came to himself again he thought over what he had learnt, and this perfect way seemed to him very grievous and burdensome, and he did not want to follow it. But he made up his mind that, in spite of this, he would try to learn the lesson which had been taught him by the good God.

It happened one day, not long after, that a lay-brother spoke to him very rudely. Henry bore it in silence and he would gladly have left it at that. But his conscience gave him no rest until he had carried out the instructions of the Eternal Wisdom. So that same evening, when the brother in question was at supper in the infirmary, Henry went upstairs and stood outside the door. When, at the end of the meal, the brother who had offended him came out, Henry fell on his knees before him, saying humbly:

"I beg you, dear worthy brother, honour God in a poor man, and if I have troubled you, forgive me for God's sake."

The brother was utterly put to shame, and kneeling in his turn, cried out:

"What wonderful thing is this that you are doing? It is I who have outraged you by my villainous words. Forgive me, for God's sake."

Another time, when Henry was dining with a guest, the brother serving them spoke to him very rudely. The friar said never a word but turned to smile sweetly at him. When the brother left the room he said to his companions:

"Never in my life have I been so grossly insulted. I was deliberately rude to Father Henry just now in the guest-room, and all he did was to smile and bow so sweetly that I went red for very shame. It will always be a good lesson to me to mind my tongue and my manners."

58

CHAPTER IX

THE FLOOD

At first sight there does not appear to be much connection between Henry Suso's life of prayer and preaching on the one hand and the historical events of the time on the other; indirectly these events did affect his apostolic work, as many of the stories told about this period show.

From the time of his irregular crowning at Aachen in 1324 there had been unceasing friction between the reigning king, Lewis of Bavaria, and John XXII, the first Pope to take up official residence at Avignon. In 1324, when Suso was studying at Cologne, Lewis had been excommunicated for the first time. In 1328 the excommunicated king had caused himself to be crowned Emperor in Rome by two excommunicated bishops; after which he declared the Pope deposed and appointed an antipope of his own choosing. In 1330 the people of his kingdom, wearied of disputes, excommunications and interdicts, constrained him to make overtures of peace to the Pope; but these came to nothing and the quarrel only ended with his life, still under sentence of excommunication, in 1347.

Rudolph von Montfort, Bishop of Constance, supported the Pope against the king until 1332 when, for the last two years of his life, he transferred his loyalty to Lewis. His successor, Nicholas von Kreuzlingen, was a devoted adherent of the pope, and this had its repercussions on Henry's fortunes, for the Dominicans supported Pope and bishop and were for a time driven from the city.

In the meantime, about the years 1329–30, Henry began to preach, travelling through Swabia and Alsace and down the Rhine as far as the Netherlands. In the places where he was known people loved him; but in many places he was a stranger and, since people came in contact with so many false mystics, such as the Brethren of the Free Spirit and the Flagellants, it was natural that such people should be very chary of receiving any strange friar as a friend. Besides, Henry himself was one of those people who are always asking for trouble and he certainly got what he asked for.

Once on his journeyings he came to a small town where the people were the proud possessors of a large wooden crucifix which was reputed to be miraculous. It stood in a tiny chapel, little more than a niche by the roadside, piled round with *ex votos*, chiefly consisting of great quantities of wax for the making of candles.

In passing the place, as was but natural, Henry turned aside and entering the chapel remained there for some time praying; after which he continued on his way to the place where he was to spend the night. His devotions, however, had not been unobserved for, from a coign of vantage where she could see without being seen, a little girl of seven years old had watched his entering and leaving the chapel. Bright-eyed and curious, though a little timid of the stranger, she had taken in every detail of his appearance, and now hurried off to her home, wondering who this man in a white habit and black cloak might be.

It happened that during this very night thieves broke into the chapel and carried off all the wax. When day dawned, men and women, on their way to work in the farms or fields, and pausing according to custom to pray before the crucifix, found to their dismay that the place had been broken into and robbed. The folk were horrified; shocked at the thought of such a sacrilege committed in their village. So, just as they were, in working-clothes with tools on their shoulders, they hurried to the house of the guardian of the shrine, a leading citizen; and with them went the little girl who had been such an interested spectator of the friar's devotions on the previous day.

Arrived at their destination, they sent for the custodian of the shrine and, as happens when an excited crowd has gathered, they all began to talk at once and of course each one had a different tale to tell.

At last the citizen managed to piece together a fairly coherent account of the theft, and as soon as he could make himself heard, he asked if anyone had any more information to give. This was the chance for which the little girl had been waiting, the chance to become, for once in her life, quite an important personage. Had she not with her own eyes seen a strange man steal into the chapel in the evening quiet? Swelling with pride, she piped out:

"I know who has taken the wax."

Again the hubbub arose as the crowd pressed round the child, each one trying to ask a different question, and each one determined to get an answer. Again the custodian of the shrine with difficulty enforced silence, and calling the child to stand on the doorstep beside him, asked:

"Who took the wax? How do you know he took it?"

"It is the brother who came into town yesterday evening. I saw him kneel in the chapel for ever so long, and then he went straight into the town. He had the wax under his great cloak."

It is strange how very ready people are to believe children's tales. The little girl's story was accepted at once on its face value; and though the better educated among the crowd realised that there was not evidence enough to convict the friar, still the tale was generally believed and roused great ill will against him through all the countryside.

It was some time before the slander reached Henry's ears, who meanwhile went about his business in complete ignorance of the accusation. He was puzzled when he saw that people began to avoid him, but when at last he learnt the reason he was horrified. It was a time when all *bona fide* preachers had to be very careful of their good name; for it was difficult at first sight to distinguish them from Brethren of the Free Spirit; and the good name of the convent depended on the individuals who were sent out to preach.

Besides, there was no small risk of his being mishandled by some mischievous mob, glad of any excuse for excitement. So, as was his fashion, Henry complained familiarly and lovingly to the Eternal Wisdom.

"Since, O Lord, it is my lot to suffer, and I must needs suffer, if thou wouldst only give me ordinary sufferings, such as would not bring disgrace, I would bear them joyfully. But by destroying my good name, thou dost strike me to the heart in those things of all others which are dearest to me."

Nevertheless, he set his teeth and determined to remain in the town to endure whatever was in store for him. And so, without meaning to do so, the unworldly friar proved his innocence in the best way by remaining in the place until the gossip about him had died down.

Undoubtedly the times were hard, and though a man measured his words never so carefully, it was sometimes almost impossible to avoid being mistaken for a false mystic. Such happened at least once to Henry. He was preaching a course of Lenten sermons in Constance where a lifesize marble crucifix hung in one of the monastery churches. One day, as he was passing the place, he met some persons who begged him to come inside with them as a miraculous stream of blood was oozing from the five wounds. To refuse might give offence, so he went in with them, and going up to the crucifix found it was just as they said. As he came close to the image the falling drops splashed on to his hand.

The news spread like wildfire, and as Henry turned to leave the church he came face to face with a big crowd clamouring for news of the prodigy; in fact, they refused to let him go until he had given them an account of the whole occurrence, telling them exactly what he had seen and showing them the drops of blood which had fallen on his hand. Seeing that there was no way out of it, Henry very reluctantly complied; adding when he had finished the account:

"Mark, please, that I pronounce no judgement as to this

happening; whether or no it is of God. I leave such a judgement to those who have a right to make it."

The prodigy was of course a nine days' wonder in the whole countryside; and the tale was told and retold with variations and embellishments according to the fancy of each teller, until at last this was the version which made its way back to the town where the wonder had taken place. Some folk in the surrounding villages, jealous that the occurrence had not taken place in their own hamlet, said that the friar had pricked his finger and rubbed the blood from it on the crucifix. He hoped in this way to convince the people that the image bled miraculously, and so to draw them to hear his sermons and enrich him with their pious offerings.

For some inexplicable reason many of the townsfolk believed the lie, and were so angry at having been, as they thought, duped by the friar that Henry was obliged to leave the district. The tale spread far and wide, and everywhere he went he was received with abuse. Even those who believed in him were so overawed by the rest that they were afraid to speak in his favour.

A lady who knew him well came to advise him to get testimonies of the facts of the case from reliable eye-witnesses, so that he might carry them about with him in proof of his innocence. Henry smiled a little sadly.

"If this were all I have to suffer, and if it were God's intention that I should have no other thing to bear but this, then I would gladly ask for such a testimonial. But as a matter of fact, so much suffering of this kind falls to my lot every day that I can only leave it to God to vindicate me when he chooses."

The devil was certainly doing all in his power to hinder the good which Henry was accomplishing by his preaching and writing. When all else failed he attempted to destroy the friar's books. Once, when he had just completed a doctrinal treatise, he was returning from Strassburg to Constance travelling with one companion along the banks of the Rhine.

As this way was well known to both of them (for the friars of Constance used the river-banks as their regular highway where friendly folk often took them part of the way by boat) they were tramping along so deeply immersed either in prayer or conversation that they were wholly ignorant of the fact that at one spot the river had overflowed its banks.

Suddenly the pair found themselves struggling, immersed to the neck in the turbid swirling waters of the flood, on which they were being rapidly carried out to the river itself. Neither could swim, so Henry, with his precious manuscript in the bosom of his tunic, commended them both to God.

As the waters closed over his head, he heard a shout from the bank. A Prussian knight, who, unknown to the friars had followed them from Strassburg, saw their peril and waded in to the rescue. Henry was nearest to his hand, so seizing him as he came to the surface he swam ashore with him. Then he went in again for his companion.

Waving off the thanks and blessings of the half-drowned pair, the good knight left them to resume his journey, while the friars went to the nearest inn to dry their soaking habits.

CHAPTER X

THE PREACHER

THE history of Suso's life at this period must seem to the reader to consist of little else but a list of the untoward adventures which overtook the friar. The story of a great and famous preacher, whose name in his own day was one to conjure with, should, by ordinary standards, be an account of sermons and mass conversions; in Henry's case there is little to relate but humiliation and trouble of all kinds. This is due to a threefold reason.

In the first place the chief, sometimes the only, source of his life is his own autobiography in which, as is the way with saints, he is much more concerned with his failures than his successes. In the second place this period of his life was undoubtedly seedtime, the preparation for the great work which lay before him at Ulm, and so God sent him to the school of humiliation until it was safe to trust him with success. The action of the Master General in 1335 can only be understood in the light of what happened in the intervening years between 1330 and 1334. In the third place, Suso's greatest triumphs were never with crowds, even though he was one of the greatest preachers of the time, but with individual souls, either sinners, or those who were seeking the way to closer union with God.

This chapter begins as the last ended with an immersion.

It happened one cold winter's day that Henry was sent by his prior on a journey alone. After travelling all day without breaking his fast, and facing a cold frosty wind in an open cart, he and the driver came at last to a millpond swollen by melting snow, whose waters were lashed to waves by the east wind.

The carter was cold and tired, and so he thought to save time by driving as close as possible to the margin of the pond. But he had not reckoned with the mud; the vehicle stuck fast. The horse pulled and the yokel pushed, trying vainly to get the wheel clear of the rut. At last they succeeded in freeing it, only to overturn the whole cart with its passenger into the pool, the unfortunate friar pinned underneath. By working his way along under the cart, Henry contrived to get his head and shoulders above water, but farther than this he could not go. He was utterly unable to extricate himself and in addition he was being drawn with the vehicle down to the mill-race. As the horse had broken loose from the cart when it overturned, the carter had no means of assisting his luckless passenger.

But help was at hand, for some of the miller's men had seen the accident and rushed up to intercept the cart before it reached the race. Happily they were in time and between them managed to drag the cart to the side of the pool and right it, releasing the friar. This done, they evidently considered that no more could be expected of them; and the carter coming up with the horse at that moment, they all went their respective ways, leaving Henry to stand there with chattering teeth, half-drowned, his wet habit rapidly freezing as hard as a board.

It was obvious, even to the friar himself, that if he did not soon find shelter he must die of cold, so gathering his wits together, he set off as fast as his half-frozen limbs would allow, in the direction of a tiny hamlet standing on the brow of a nearby hill. But by this time night had fallen and the folk had barred their doors for fear of thieves; so that it was vain for the friar to wander from one end of the single street to the other, knocking at every door, for no one would open to him.

At last he turned back the way he had come, intending to see if he could find shelter in one of the mill barns, but his strength gave way and he could go no farther; so crouched in the lee of one of the cottages he began to cry aloud to God in his own fashion, sure of being heard:

"O Lord! It would have been better for me if thou hadst allowed me to die by drowning, for then there would have been an end of it, instead of my being frozen to death in this street."

The man of the house heard his prayer, and moved with pity opened the door to help the friar inside. There he settled down before the hearth, as his host directed, to endure as best he might the agony of returning circulation. Still all was well with him for he says:

66

To suffer for the love of God is perfect happiness; at first mortification appears hard and cruel, but by little and little it loses its bitterness and becomes exceeding sweet.

And again:

Souls devoured by zeal in God's service desire to suffer death itself to advance his glory, and in order to learn his holy will. . . . Since the beginning of the world, love of God has inflamed his followers, has drawn them to seek and desire God's good pleasure. Happy, a thousand times happy, he who knows him, and knowing him and following him hears his voice and never leaves his holy path.

And from the *Little Book of Eternal Wisdom*:

If suffering gave no pain it could not be called suffering. There is nothing more painful than suffering, nothing more joyful than to have suffered. Suffering is a short pain and a long joy. Suffering gives pain to the sufferer here and joy hereafter. Suffering kills suffering. Suffering is ordained that the sufferer may not suffer eternally. Hadst thou as much spiritual sweetness and divine consolation, and heavenly delight as at all times to run over with heavenly dew, it would not be so very meritorious for thee in itself; since for all this together I would not have to thank thee so much, it would not exculpate thee so much as a loving suffering, or patience in adversity which thou sufferest for my sake. . . . If thou hadst as much science as all astronomers, if thou couldst discourse as well of God as all the tongues of men and angels, and didst possess the treasure of knowledge of all masters, not all this would avail to advance thee in a good life as much as if thou gavest thyself up and didst leave thyself to God's will in all thy sufferings; for the former is common to the good and bad, but this is proper to my elect alone.

The fruits of his preaching and penances were very great, for there were numbers of sinners whom the friar converted about this time. There was, among others, a ferocious man who had not been to the Sacraments for eighteen years; and at another time twelve women of evil life, whose conversion afterwards caused him endless trouble and annoyance, and

67

of these twelve only two persevered to the end. There were many other women who had fallen into sin whom he saved from despair and perhaps suicide. Once terrible trouble befell him and of this he received warning from God beforehand.

He was told by his superiors to take up his headquarters in a certain town and from there to preach through the surrounding district. On his way there he stopped for the night at an inn, and falling asleep, it seemed to him that he was prepared to sing mass. As he went up the altar steps, the choir began the *officium* for the Mass of Martyrs.

"*Multae tribulationes justorum,*" they sang, and Henry thought within himself that this was very strange for it was not the feast of any martyr. He did not want to hear of the many tribulations of the just, so turning to the choir he said rather sharply:

"We are keeping no martyrs' feast to-day. Why then are you deafening us with martyrs? Why sing the martyrs' Proper?"

But the choir pointing to him answered: "God has his martyrs now, as he has always had; get ready and sing for thyself."

But the friar was in no mood for martyrdom, so he began to turn over the pages of the missal, looking for the Mass of Confessors, or of Virgins, or of any other except that of Martyrs; but he could find no other masses in the book save only that of Martyrs. So he began to sing rather sadly as he was obliged to do. But he found it so difficult that presently he turned again to the choir and said:

"This is strange; for people would much rather sing *Gaudeamus* about joyful things than *Multae tribulationes* as you are doing."

And the choir answered: "Do you not understand yet? This song about martyrs comes first and then, when the proper time has come, the joyful song *Gaudeamus* follows after."

68

Then Henry awoke, saying sorrowfully: "Alas, my God! Must I once more suffer martyrdom?"

CHAPTER XI

THE SURRENDER

THE town to which Friar Henry was sent to preach was somewhere in the neighbourhood of his own home. It could not have been Strassburg with its dream-lovely Gothic cathedral, for there he would have stayed in the Dominican priory instead of lodging in the town. This place, wherever it might be, stood on the banks of the Rhine, and it must have been of some importance since it was built at a place where a great bridge spanned the river.

Henry began at once to preach, and it was not long before his sermons drew great crowds. Many of those who heard him came afterwards to visit him at his lodging, to ask for advice and help. Among those who flocked to hear the preacher, drawn by the novelty and excitement, was a woman who was about as bad as she could be. Outwardly respectable, and contriving somehow to preserve her reputation, she lived, nevertheless, the life of a woman about the streets. She had a child, too, though until that time she had kept the secret of its existence to herself. At the time when Henry came to the town she was having a hard struggle to make ends meet, and when she laid eyes on the friar, marking his simplicity and utter unworldliness, she came to the conclusion that she had found a gold mine.

One of two things, she thought, was bound to happen; either she would hoodwink this visionary by pretended

69

repentance, or she would somehow lead him into sin and then she could blackmail him to her heart's content. These begging friars had long purses, but it would go hard with her if, in one way or another, she did not bleed him white.

So after she had watched him carefully from the back of the crowd, and made her own estimate of his character, she followed him to his lodging with the most convincing story of a penitent magdalen. She began by confessing her sins, and, with bold appraising eyes watching his face, she did not minimise matters.

At first Henry was completely taken in. He did not like the woman, his instincts were all against her; but he was on his master's business seeking the lost sheep, so he set his teeth to endure the stench of sin and to do his best for the woman. She, on her part, listened to his exhortations and promised a complete change of life. But, she said, she was so poor, so poor, and what was a poor soul to do but earn her bread as best she might, when the wolf was at the door, and her innocent babe was crying for hunger. Henry gave her money, and if she would only keep her resolutions, promised her more; want should not drive her to sin if he could help it.

But, said the woman, she was weak and temptations such as she had yielded to took such a hold that without help and spiritual strengthening she was lost. Might she come from time to time to see him for her poor soul's sake? Surely she might. One last favour she asked, might she come in the evening when all was quiet; if people saw her on her way to the friar they might guess her secret? Let her come when she would, Henry would help her.

For nine or ten months she kept up her deception, while the friar came backwards and forwards from town to countryside on his journeys; and then suddenly he found her out. Perhaps he met her one night as he was returning home late; perhaps someone told him. But, however he learnt it, the knowledge was sufficient to decide him to have nothing more to do with her, and so he told her he would have her no more at his lodgings, neither would he see her or speak with her elsewhere.

At first she was furious, and left him threatening vengeance. But when she considered the matter in her own room later, she decided that things might be worse and that the time had now come to try the second string to her bow. She had never come within striking distance of his virtue but, with a little management on her part, his reputation was in her hands. She had been to his lodging and people had seen her.

She hurried there now, knocked at the door, and when he opened it, thrust her foot into the gap so that he could not close it. Then she gave the friar his ultimatum. With much evil language she told him that he could either continue his charity as he had until then—for his exhortations she cared nothing, he was welcome to omit these—or, she had a new-born babe at her home and she would tell all the world that it was his.

She stepped back and Henry closed the door in her face, then he sat down to consider his dilemma. If she kept her threat what had he best do? He, a comparatively young man, had been trusted alone on missionary work; how would his superiors think that he had justified the trust put in him? This woman had been to his lodgings more than once, and she had it in her hands to blast his reputation. But after all, what was his reputation? The only thing that really mattered was the reality of his life as he stood in the sight of God. To guard his reputation would be to fail in his devoir to his Spouse, the Eternal Wisdom; therefore the only thing to do was to leave his honour in God's hands, where it was safe. So he settled himself to his prayers.

The woman kept her word; and so furious was she at her failure to bend Henry to her will that, in having her revenge, she did not hesitate to ruin her own reputation. She went from one person to another; from ecclesiastics to seculars, from magistrates to merchants; and everywhere she blazoned it abroad that she had a new-born child, and that Friar Henry was its father.

The tale was believed, for evil is more readily accepted than good; and to add to the reality of the tale the woman left the baby at the friar's lodgings. Henry found a decent woman to foster the child, and held his tongue, hoping to prove his innocence by ignoring the slander and going about his business as if gossiping tongues were not busy. But it was all to no purpose. It was not long before the tale reached the foster-mother's ears, and she came to his lodging one day in a high state of indignation. The friar was a saint, she knew it, and as innocent of worldly wisdom and wickedness as the babe she was nursing.

"There must be an end of this," quoth she. "The town is ringing with lies now, but if the babe was gone, gossip would soon die down. None but a fool or a saint would have left it here so long. The river is near, and 'twould be easy to slip on the bank some dark night and lose the baby. Nay"—as she saw the expression on the other's face—"if you are overnice for such work, let me leave it in the church early one morning. 'Tis not the first foundling left to chance charity and none the worse for it."

Henry rose with a white blazing face.

"Woman," he cried, "do you wish me to make an innocent child suffer for the sins of its mother? As I hope for mercy myself I will be merciful and care for it. Since its own mother has abandoned it, with God's help I will provide for it. Let me know what it costs you, and somehow I will find the money." He paused a moment, and then added in gentler tones: "Bring the child here secretly; I wish to see it."

Quite conquered and subdued, the woman left in tearful silence, and one night soon after brought the child to the friar's lodging. He took the baby from her and the little one, lying in his arms, smiled up at him so that he could do

72

no other but smile back at it. He caressed it, saying: "Child of my heart, why should you die because you are not mine but have cost me much pain? My beautiful, dear, tender child, I will not hurt you, but will take care of you, for you are God's child and mine too. So long as God gives me a single mouthful, I will share it with you to the glory of God; and I will bear patiently whatever may happen to me on your account, dear little child."

The woman who had been standing by watching the friar with the baby in his arms, was moved to tears.

"May God bless you!" she cried. "Give me the baby and think no more of it, for I will bring it up as one of my own."

Henry looked keenly at the speaker, and, seeing that she was to be trusted, he put the child back in her arms, blessing it and saying:

"May the loving God bless thee and the holy angels guard thee from all evil. Give it all that it needs and I will pay you," he added to the woman.

All this time the child's mother had continued her lying tales, acting on the principle that if sufficient mud is thrown some of it is sure to stick. The gossip soon reached the ears of the friar's kinsfolk living in the neighbourhood, making them furiously angry. One went to see him, to tell him with great indignation:

"This must stop, for 'tis simply monstrous that an ill-famed woman should use you in this way; not only on your own account but for the sake of your kin. I will post myself this evening in the middle of the bridge, for she crosses it each nightfall. Then I will throw her in the river, and no one the wiser. As for the wretch herself, I consider it a good action to rid the world of such vermin."

Was Henry for a moment sharply tempted? Did he think how good it would be thus to shuffle so easily out of his trouble without himself raising a finger? Surely the thought must have passed through his mind; but whether or no it

73

did, his outward reaction was swift. Turning on his kinsman, he cried out:

"God, who knows all hidden things, knows that the woman has done me wrong about this child, therefore I will leave the matter in his hands, either to slay her or let her live according to his will."

But his visitor was not inclined to relinquish his purpose so easily. The scandal was inconveniencing the whole family, so he argued the point again and again until at last Henry said decisively:

"Think no more on it, but let all sufferings fall on me that God wishes me to suffer."

Courage and patience cannot altogether still heartache, and as the tide of gossip rose, battering against the one possession which the friar held dear—his good name—Henry arrived at such an extremity of suffering that, being, as he was, alone and separated from his community, he was driven at last to seek help and comfort from old friends of his, men whose friendship had meant a great deal to him. But they too turned their backs on him, telling him bluntly that they no longer wished to have anything to do with a man who was the common talk of the district. They valued their own reputation too highly, they said, to risk being seen in the company of a man of whose acquaintance they were ashamed.

One of them said to him scoffingly: "This is an end of you and your books and your preaching."

The friar was hurt but he answered quietly:

"I put my trust in the good God of heaven that, when the appointed time shall come, my books will be yet more valued and loved than they have ever been." And turning away, he went back to his solitude.

Since he had made his headquarters in the town, kindhearted folk had seen to it that Henry wanted for nothing; but now that everyone was talking about him, these no longer gave him alms, and so for a time being dependent on charity, the friar was literally in want. In time these people came to learn the truth and repented their want of charity, but for some while longer his good name continued to be the sport of evil tongues. The story of his supposed disgrace was carried far and wide even by persons esteemed for their piety. These told the tale with a wealth of sanctimoniously regretful phrases, professing their friendship for the friar and their sorrow at his fall; which manner of telling did him far more harm than any open abuse could have done.

So far Henry had comforted himself with the thought that his own Order at least had not condemned him; but now he had this consolation no longer, for one day while travelling he heard that the Master General and the Provincial had gone to the town where his trouble had begun. He felt this to be the last straw, for he could not see how his superiors, hearing, as they were bound to hear, all the tales that were current about him, even among persons of good judgement and high position, could help believing him guilty. The offence of which he was accused was most serious, and it seemed to him that they could do no other than expel him from the Order he so dearly loved.

Temptations to despair, temptations to question God's love and goodness, temptations to rebel against his hard fate, weighed him down until he felt literally crushed under the load. He could not rest, he could not even remain still, he could not concentrate on his work or prayer. He was capable of nothing but tramping up and down his small room, hoping to weary his body so far that fatigue might for a time make him forget. For half a day he paced ceaselessly up and down, wrestling with pain and temptation until at last, the victory won, he lifted his battered soul to God in one supreme act of trust and love.

"*Fiat voluntas tua*," he cried.

Swiftly the answer came. First he heard that the woman who had been the primary cause of all his trouble had died suddenly. Not many days after he heard that the Master General and the Provincial, having held a most careful inquiry into the scandal, completely exculpated him. They declared publicly that they had found nothing against him except that a woman whose evil life made her word utterly untrustworthy had spoken maliciously of an honest man; a thing which may well happen when people give ear to evil tongues.

So the friar's griefs were turned to joys, and he was gladdened by inward peace of heart, still repose and the bright illuminations of grace. Surely it was in the light of this experience that Henry once preached to his brethren, saying:

When Jesus Christ wished to leave his followers a simple and sure way to heaven, a road which should be short, straight and certain, he said to them: "I came forth from the Father and am come into the world; again I leave the world and go to the Father." I came from the bosom, the heart, of my Father, I came into this valley of tears where I was daily oppressed with sorrows and miseries, numberless and measureless. And this I endured willingly for your salvation. I did not give myself so much as one hour for rest or pleasure; I refused all the comforts and joys of life; I was arrested and condemned to death, crucified and buried. But afterwards I rose, glorious and impassible; I returned in triumph to the bosom of my Father, to share with him his eternity of bliss.

You, my dearly beloved, must follow the same path. Let no one deceive himself. In order to reign with me in the bosom of my Father, in order to become impassible, immortal, to gain heaven, the heritage of joy which is mine by nature and will be yours by grace, every one must suffer, die and be buried with me. Certainly, my brethren, Jesus Christ could not better assure us of heaven than by inviting us to imitate his sorrowful life, his death and his burial. As Saint Paul says: "For we are buried with him by baptism unto death; that, as Christ is risen from the dead by the glory of the Father, so also we may walk in newness of life. For, if we have been planted together in the likeness of his death, so shall we also be in the likeness of his resurrection." Happy the servant of God who walks in the newness of life in this way of death and burial with Christ. Truly it can be said of him that he is as far above the man of the world as men of the world, by their human nature, are above the brute creation.

CHAPTER XII

THE SISTER

THE web of human history is woven of intermingled good and evil. And as in a tapestry when strong colours are used the contrasts are more vivid, so when good is at its best and brightest, all evil is also at its worst and blackest. It is like a day of mingled cloud and sunshine; when the sun is hidden everything takes on a uniform grey shade, but when it comes out from behind the cloud, then light is sparkling silver and shadow of the deepest black. South Germany in the days of Friar Henry was passing through a time of silver and black.

There was no choice of career in those days for the daughters of the nobility—their destiny hung between marriage and the cloister. Most fathers married off their daughters as long as funds lasted, then the remainder went into convents. This was, of course, by no means the invariable rule, for many a maiden, conscious that she had a religious vocation, braved all sorts of difficulties in carrying it out; but there were many more who became nuns simply because it was the accepted alternative to marriage. As a result of this there were two classes of convents: houses of strict observance for the fervent, and houses where, the rule being more honoured in the breach than the observance, the lax could live almost as comfortably as if they were in their own homes. Many of these convents were not enclosed, and as there was not the same opportunity as now for works of active charity, Satan found plenty of mischief for idle hands.

Henry Suso had a sister who was a nun in such a monastery. She might have been sent there very young, since it was the custom for the daughters of nobles to be educated in convents where they often remained later as religious. This particular monastery was far from being what it should; and as the child grew up, little by little she drifted into careless habits. She loved the world and its pleasures and so she lost no opportunity of paying visits about the town. It is not difficult to conjecture what is most likely to happen when an ignorant, frivolous and innocent girl follows her wayward will with little or no supervision. After a while she fell into grievous sin. Her next action was also what might be expected of ignorance and foolishness.

Horrified at herself and frightened to death, overwhelmed with shame and not knowing where she could go for help, the silly girl put on secular clothes and ran away. She had absolutely no experience of fending for herself, and so was at her wits' end what to do for food and shelter. She dared not return to her home, neither did she dare go to her brother the friar; and so with a kind of pitiful simplicity she decided that there was nothing for her to do but to dress herself up in the gaudy rags of a courtesan and find a living in the streets.

Henry was absent from his priory at the time when this happened, but on his return it was not long before one or other of his brethren told him the tale. For a while he was stunned by the shock; for, in addition to his distress in hearing of her sin and shame, he dearly loved this little sister of his, and his trouble was no easier because no one could tell him what had become of her after she had run away.

He set to work at once to make enquiries, but for some time he could learn nothing. He was, of course, acutely conscious of the disgrace and he used to fancy that when he went up to speak to the other friars they drew back from him in disgust. So sensitive did he become that at last it became a matter of real difficulty to join the community in choir or refectory. When it dawned on him that he was playing a coward's part he pulled himself together, saying to himself:

"A new suffering is quite right, though it is hard that it should have taken this shape. Do not lose heart, Henry, but see if you cannot find this poor sister of yours and bring her home. Offer at once the sacrifice of your worldly honour to a merciful God; cast aside all human shame; spring after her into the pit and draw her out." Calling to mind the saying of Job, he comforted himself saying: "The compassionate God must needs strengthen me, since all the world has left me."

At length word was brought to him that the girl was to be found in a certain village, and so, on January the twentieth, he set out to find her.

The weather was raw, damp and chilly, much rain had fallen on the previous night, and it was not long before the friar found himself ploughing his way through heavy marshy ground intersected with runnels. When he awoke to the fact of his whereabouts, he looked round him in some dismay. This was not the first time that his habit of absorption had led him into difficulties. To go back was as bad as to go on, he must make the best of it. So he dragged his weary way through the mud, jumping the little brooks in his path. At one he miscalculated his distance, and fell in. That also, he considered ruefully as he picked himself up and looked at his soaked, mud-plastered habit, was quite in accordance with what might have been expected of him.

At last, in sorry plight, he reached the hamlet for which he was bound and made his way to the village inn, a poor enough place, little better than a hovel. In answer to his enquiry, one of the men lounging at the door told him that there was a girl inside; so he made his way into the one living-room of the place.

There she sat, poor little soul, on a bench by the smoky fire, the garish tawdriness of her dress in pathetic contrast to her scared white child's face. As he stood at the door, peering at her through the mist of smoke, the pity, the pathos and the incongruity almost broke her brother's heart. This was the sister whom he loved and with whom he had played when they were children together.

She was staring into the red heart of the fire and did not see him as he softly crossed the room and seated himself on the bench at her side. Speech was impossible to him, and so he sat there in silence and waited.

Suddenly the girl became aware that she was no longer alone, and glancing round hastily, she came face to face with her brother. Startled and frightened, she rose with a cry and tried to run away, but she was trembling so that she could do nothing but drop back again on to the seat and cover her face with her hands.

Henry remained so still beside her that at last she gained courage enough to look timidly in his direction. His face was terribly sad, but it did not look scornful or angry; could it be possible that there was some hope for her after all? She slid off the bench on her knees at his feet. Then, as he neither moved nor spoke, nor made any attempt to draw away from her, she began to speak in a whisper.

"I have sinned. I have sinned against God and my vows. I have disgraced our name. I have disgraced you. I am sorry; I was really sorry all the time, but I was afraid. I did not know what to do. I know it is not right that you should call me your sister. But, for Jesus' sake, help me as you would help any other sinner. Find a way to give me one more chance. I am not afraid of a penance." Her voice died away, and for a time brother and sister wept together. At last Henry found voice to speak to her.

"Since I have found my child, I will weep no more; and I will receive her to-day with the same love and pity with which I pray the merciful God to receive me, a sinful creature, when it is time for me to die. My dear, I gladly forgive you the great pain and sorrow which you have caused me, even though the ache must remain to my life's end. I will help you to the uttermost of my power to expiate your sin, that you may regain your good name in the sight of God and men."

Crouched on the ground the girl continued to sob bitterly.

"Now come with me," said Henry. And she rose at once and followed him from the house.

The task he had set himself was no easy one. First he had to persuade some discreet woman to give the girl lodging until he had obtained from her ecclesiastical superiors absolution from the double breach of her vows. When this was accomplished, he applied to her former community to readmit her. But they would have none of it. She had left them of her own accord, raising a scandal in which they were involved. They had been most straitly questioned, and censured too, for not taking better care of their young nuns. Friar Henry must understand, once and for all, that they would on no account take her back.

At his wits' end Henry betook himself to the superioress of a fervent community, without, however, much hope of accomplishing anything. But, to his surprise, the superioress agreed to give the girl a trial. Henry's own reputation stood so high that she was sure there must be good in his sister. Besides, she probably knew the reputation of the convent from which the girl had run away.

Full of gratitude to God and to the charitable religious, Henry took his sister to her new home. There she made good; and after a life spent in the fervent service of God, she died a most holy and happy death.

CHAPTER XIII

THE PRIOR

THE year 1334 saw the culmination of Friar Henry's troubles. He had been warned of this when our Lord called him from corporal to spiritual penance. He was told then that his sufferings would come from three sources: there would be mortifications inflicted by others; he would suffer dereliction; and he would be deprived of all spiritual consolations. Then, and only then, would God's knight be perfected in all knightly exercises. The training of the Minnesinger would be complete, and the lyre of divine wisdom would be tuned to play the song of divine love.

One day when, according to his custom, he was praying in his oratory begging of God to teach him how to suffer, Jesus Christ appeared to him in the form of a seraph on a cross. This seraph had six wings; with two he covered his head, with two he covered his feet, and with two he flew. On the two wings covering his feet was written: AFFLICTIONEM SPONTE SUSCIPE—Receive sufferings willingly, as though his Master bade the friar run to meet suffering. On the two wings with which the seraph flew was written: FERAS CRUCEM AEQUANIMITER—Carry the cross in patience, for of a surety, sufferings are the wings on which a soul flies to God. On the pair of wings which covered the head was written: DISCE PATI CHRISTIFORMITER—Learn to suffer after Christ's pattern, since suffering gains its value from the conformity of the will.

These are the three degrees in the perfection of suffering; prompt submission of the will; unruffled calm whether God sends good or evil fortune; and the endurance of suffering in union with the charity of Christ.

Wishing to learn the meaning of this vision, Henry went

to a dear friend, one versed in the mysteries of God, and asked him what was in store. Said his friend:

"The vision means that new sufferings are to come upon you."

"In what will these sufferings consist?" asked the friar.

"You are going to be elected prior of the house at Constance," he was told, "and this is to give those people who dislike you fresh opportunities of wounding you."

It happened at that time that there was a succession of lean years with bad harvests, and so there was great scarcity of food in the district. People could no longer give the friars alms, there was no provision in the store-rooms and the community very often went hungry. Added to this the house was heavily in debt.

In the midst of this trouble the prior's term of office came to an end and the friars began to discuss whom they should elect in his place. Someone was needed, said they, who would draw crowds to the priory church to fill both granary and almsboxes. After all, Henry the Dreamer was a well-known and popular preacher, with a host of well-to-do friends; he would answer this particular purpose better than anyone else. So they elected Henry Suso as their new prior.

Taken at its best the office of superior is a heavy, distasteful burden, but when, as in Henry's case, the prior-elect knows perfectly well that he has been chosen simply for convenience's sake, the weight becomes well-nigh insupportable. However, since such was God's will, he accepted office without making any demur.

On the day of his installation he caused the bell to be rung summoning the friars to chapter, and there he made an exhortation.

Saint Dominic, he said, had promised his sons that he would be more useful to them after death than during his life; and so, in their present dire need, the only thing they could do was to remind their Father of his promise. For this end, on the following morning a votive mass should be sung. He would sing it.

The friars looked at each other in dismay, for this was not at all what they had hoped for or expected. If they had been in the new prior's place, there would have been talk of plans for beginning a fresh course of sermons, coupled with suggestions of appeals to be made to all his wealthy friends. They were without food or money and there were plenty of wealthy folk who would willingly respond to Prior Henry's request for help. Now all that the dreamer had suggested was an additional burden of prayer, as if they had not been storming heaven for months already. Heaven helps those who help themselves. Two of the most disappointed even turned and began muttering to each other.

"What a fool! He can do no more than bid us turn to Saint Dominic. Does he fancy that heaven will open, and that meat and drink will fall in showers on us?"

"He's not the only fool. We were fools every whit as bad for having made him our prior, though we knew quite well that he is ignorant of earthly things, and does nothing but gape continually up to heaven."

Next morning after mass, as the new prior was kneeling in prayer the porter came to call him to the guest quarters. There he found a friend of his, one of his converts, a wealthy canon of the town. The canon greeted the prior with twinkling eyes, for he had made a shrewd guess as to where his difficulties would most likely lie.

"Father prior," he said, "I know that you are not exactly a man of business. It seems that God Almighty knows this also, for last night he put it into my mind to be his almoner. So, for a beginning, I have brought you this twenty pounds weight of Constance pennies. Put your trust in God as you have always done, for he will never forsake you."

It was the turn of the community to look a little foolish when, an hour or two later, their Prior returned from the town, bringing with him provisions—corn and wine—

sufficient to last them for a long time. And this was not the only occasion when Saint Dominic came to their help, for during the two years that Henry was prior alms came in so abundantly that the procurator was able to feed the whole convent without drawing on the priory revenues, and to pay the outstanding debt as well.

But our friar seemed born to trouble as the sparks fly upward. Not long after this his friend the canon died, and on his deathbed sent for him. After settling his spiritual affairs the dying man gave the other a great number of silver florins, telling him to distribute them at his discretion to pious people—beguines, hermits and the like—who had grown old in the service of God and in their old age were in need of help. Henry did not at all relish this commission, for he foresaw that it could lead to nothing but trouble. At last, however, after holding out for some time, he yielded to the dying man's importunity and took the money. The canon died soon after, and the prior's troubles, as he had foreseen, began almost immediately.

Among the canon's heirs was a dissolute young man, who soon came to the end of his own large legacy, and finding himself in difficulties betook himself to the prior, demanding the sum which had been given him for charitable purposes, and threatening to kill him if he refused. The young man was quite capable of carrying out his threat, and it received additional weight from the fact that, shortly before, a friar had actually been murdered by thieves who knew he had alms in his possession.

Henry was of a naturally timid disposition, and it cost him no small effort to continue his work; but his provincial approved and directed his almsgiving and so, in spite of threats, he continued to carry out the provisions of the canon's will. Before very long, however, relief came to him, for the young man died suddenly.

But even so, Henry had not reached the end of his troubles regarding the unlucky legacy. He kept a minute account of the way in which he spent the money, to whom he gave and how much, sending a copy of the account from time to time to his provincial. Among others of the canon's beneficiaries was a college of ecclesiastics to whom he left a great sum of money. But they did not consider their legacy sufficient, and so they applied to Henry for some of the money left in trust to him for the poor, on the plea that they too complied with the conditions of the bequest.

This he could not agree to, and his refusal made them furious. So, by way of revenge, they broadcast a whole tissue of lies concerning the people to whom the prior had given money, his relations with them and his reasons for helping them. He paid no heed to their slanders and continued with the distribution of the legacy; nevertheless, these tales spread far and wide and did him great harm.

Just when all these difficulties were at their height, the canon one night appeared in vision to Henry, wearing a beautiful green vestment embroidered with red roses. He told his friend that he was in heaven and begged him to bear in patience the great wrong that was being done him, for that God, in his own good time, would reward him a hundredfold.

"What is the meaning of the vestment you are wearing?" asked Henry.

"The red roses on the green ground are the patient sufferings with which you have richly clothed me; and for this God will clothe you everlastingly with himself. Neither shall my protection ever be wanting to you." This promise was abundantly fulfilled.

After Henry had been prior for a year, the Provincial Chapter of the German Province was held at Bois-le-duc. There certain of the friars declared that his latest treatise, *The Book of Truth*, contained heresy. The charge could not have been substantiated to the satisfaction of the Capitular Fathers, for though Henry was severely reprimanded for what they may have considered as rash statements, and was even threatened with punishment, he was not absolved from the office of prior, as would have certainly happened if anything had been really proved against his teaching.

Some time after this, for several nights in succession, Henry was awakened from sleep by hearing these words repeated in his ears: "O God, my God! Look upon me; far from my salvation are the words of my sins," and so on for the whole of the psalm used in offices of the Cross and Passion. Henry understood the meaning, and though he shrank in fear, still his will cried to God.

" My Lord and God, if I must suffer a new crucifixion accomplish in me, a poor man, I beseech thee, thy pure and innocent death. Be with me and help me to be victorious in my sufferings."

In the year 1335 the general chapter was held at Bruges under the Master General, Hugh de Vaucimain, and Henry was absolved from office. As he was placed in no other important position, this step must be regarded as a censure; or perhaps the reasons for it were merely prudential. In the previous year he had been accused of heretical expressions in his writings. He had also been in trouble in the matter of a legacy. Some years before, the Master General on his Visitation had made strict enquiries concerning a very grave scandal which had been circulated. Now, though he had been completely exonerated each time, his superiors may well have considered it unwise to allow a prior possessing such an unfortunate faculty for attracting unfavourable notice to continue in office.

Henry's feelings at this disgrace must have been mixed. While it was a great joy to him to be free of the burden of superiority, the manner in which he was relieved must have caused great pain. Human nature is the same in saints as in sinners; and a man values his honour above everything else. He found in the course of his life that such sufferings are God's best gifts, for no man is truly free until he has learnt that nothing matters except God and his love, and this supreme lesson can only be learnt through humiliation. He found it a hard lesson and to master it brought him almost to death's door.

One night when he was away from home staying in the house of one of his true friends, a man whom he had rescued from a life of sin, when he went up to his bed a great weakness and fainting came on him; he grew cold and rigid, and his pulse was so feeble that it could not be felt. His friend, kneeling beside the bed, thought that he had really died and began the prayers for a departed soul. The friar remained thus, apparently dead for about a quarter of an hour; and then he rose quite suddenly completely restored to health.

Whilst he had lain there, his bodily senses and powers inactive, his soul had been keenly and deeply alive, wrapt in contemplation of God and the Godhead, Truth itself in indwelling and everlasting oneness.

O everlasting Truth, he prayed, thy deep abysses are hidden from every creature. I, thy poor servant, know by my deathly weakness that I am come to my end. Therefore, on the threshold of eternity, I speak to thee, mighty God, whom no one can deceive. Thou alone knowest how things stand between me and thee; therefore, I seek mercy from thee, my heavenly Father. Wherever I have broken out into unlikeness of, and defection from the supreme Truth, I grieve for it and repent with my whole heart. I beseech thee, blot it out with thy precious Blood, in accordance with thy gracious goodness and my needs.

Remember, I pray, that all the days of my life I have celebrated and exalted as highly as I could thy pure and innocent Blood. Grant that at my departure from life it may wash me from my sins. I entreat you, all ye saints, especially thou, my kind and gracious lord, Saint Nicholas, lift up your hearts with me to beseech the Lord for a good end. O pure, gentle, kind Mother Mary, reach me thy hand to-day, and at this my last hour, graciously receive my soul beneath thy sheltering mantle, for thou art my heart's joy and consolation. O Lady, Mother mine, into thy hands I commend my spirit. Dear angels, be mindful that all my life my heart has ever laughed within me if

I only heard you named; and forget not how often you have brought me heavenly joys in my sorrows and guarded me from my foes. O gentle Spirits, it is now, when my greatest straits have come, that I am in greatest need of your help. Help me, then, and shield me from the horrible sight of my foes, the evil spirits.

O Lord of Heaven, I praise thee for having bestowed on me at my death-hour full consciousness, for I go hence in the full Christian faith, without a doubt and without a fear. I forgive all who have ever made me suffer, as thou upon thy Cross forgavest those who crucified you. Lord, let thy divine Sacramental Body, which I, a sick man, received at mass to-day, be my guardian and convoy to thy divine countenance. My last prayer which I now make, gentle Lord of Heaven, is for my dear spiritual children who, whether by special bonds of faithfulness or through confession, have lovingly attached themselves to me. O merciful God, as thou at thy departure didst commend thy dear disciples to thy heavenly Father, even so, in the selfsame love, let these be commended to thee, and grant them also a good and holy end. And now I turn myself altogether away from creatures, to turn myself wholly to the pure Godhead, the primal Fountainhead of everlasting bliss.

And, his prayer being ended, he fell into ecstasy and all his sensitive faculties were suspended while God lifted his soul to rest awhile in him.

Constance being an imperial city naturally took an active part in the party politics of the time. During the last two years of his life its bishop, Rudolph von Montfort, had supported the king, Lewis of Bavaria, against the Pope. His successor, Nicholas von Kreuzlingen, consecrated in 1344, upheld the papal power. The Dominicans of Constance were staunch in their loyalty to the Pope, and so, in 1339, the magistrates of the city drove the friars from their home. They took refuge in a little town not far distant called Deissenhoven. While in exile the office of prior again falling vacant, the community remembered all that Henry had done for them by his goodness and his prayers, and so they elected him prior again; this time, however, for his moral worth and not merely for expediency. It was during this second term of office that the community returned to Constance. It ended in 1343 and in 1346 he was sent to Ulm where he remained until his death, reaping in joy the fruit of what he had sown in tears.

We have no other direct information as to what occurred during this period, but he has left a letter of counsel addressed to one of his friends who was elected prior; and as saints first practise what they preach we may be certain that he has given a word-picture of the ideal that he set before himself.

It is very evident, my dear father, that he who withdraws himself from obedience makes an insupportable burden of his life. The little that he actually does despite himself is harder and more difficult than painful things which he might do with love and eagerness. Receive then, the charge that God lays on you and fulfil it in such a way as neither to offend your Master nor wound your own conscience. I can assure you that in an office of this kind neither annoyances nor distasteful duties are lacking. For one thing, even among those from whom you ought to receive submission, you will often meet with difficulties, even insubordination. Those who conscientiously fulfil the office of prior in these days ought not to look for rest, but must expect weariness and annoyance, a life of bitterness and misery. So then, for the love of Christ Jesus, take up this cross and do not excuse yourself from carrying it on the grounds of weakness and incapacity. Rather must you weary yourself out under the weight of the charge, striving always to do what seems to you the best and most perfect thing. We fulfil our duty most perfectly by refusing to follow the timid suggestions of our sensitive natures.

In all such matters consider the service of God rather than your temporal advantage; and in enforcing the observance of the monastic rule show yourself the same to all. To be as severe with your friends as with those who oppose you is the secret of peace. Be firm with the young friars, because badly disciplined juniors are the ruin of the monastic state. Be grave and modest, certainly, but at the same time gentle and affable, so that you may be more loved than feared. Act so that obedience is given more from love than from fear.

When called upon to deal with matters that are beyond the

scope of your jurisdiction have recourse to your higher superiors. And as for abuses, though you must not countenance them, if you cannot get rid of them at least raise yourself above them. If you cannot bring back primitive observance, you can at least ensure that there is no further relaxation. Just as a friar's old and torn habit, if unmended, will soon be in ribbons, so where spiritual things are neglected, little by little temporal ones will fail.

Lead those under you by good example rather than by exhortation. In carrying out a duty it is impossible to please everybody without offending God and sinning against truth, so, when you have done what you conceive to be your duty with a good intention, if your efforts do not meet with success, and those whom you have served tear your motives to shreds and load you with ingratitude, bear all with patience remembering that the glory of the saints is the contempt and ill-will of the world. Take care that there are no scandalmongers in the priory, and that no cabals are formed there. Watch above all with the greatest care to break off all dangerous friendships, that is, in so far as your ability and prudence permit. Notice what happens in priories and convents where these two abuses, namely, gossiping cliques and dangerous friendships, are found; the first destroys all peace and the second dishonours the rest of the community.

But, you may say to yourself, if I carry out all these prescriptions I shall have to turn everything upside down, and upset all existing arrangements. I tell you: it is a happy disturbance which will be the source of everlasting peace. Does not Jeremias refer to feeble and pliable superiors, those whose one desire is to avoid reproaches and live in quietude, when he says: "And they healed the breach of the daughter of my people disgracefully saying: Peace, peace, and there was no peace"? Such superiors will sell their good-will to their subjects; they delight in temporal honours, and they buy these by sacrificing the constitutions and the sanctity of the priory. But woe to them! They have received their reward.

Do not follow such examples, but always keep as your end the honour, glory and praise of God. In this you will follow the example of Jesus Christ who, in obedience to and for glorification of his Father suffered himself to be nailed to the Cross. Perhaps your desire is for a little quiet in order to study, meditate and give yourself to contemplation; but, says Saint Gregory, he who is invested with an office must consecrate himself to the active life, and may only give himself to contemplation as far as, and never any further than, his work will permit. You may perhaps have to suffer weariness and fatigue of mind and body, but why should you complain? Is your body torn with wounds? Is your face covered with blood like those of the holy martyrs at that time when only the most perfect and courageous, those who never sought their own good, were raised to dignities?

That which I commend to you above all else is true humility. An interior knowledge of your own littleness is a great good. It is good for you to know the nothingness of your own powers, the miseries of your body and the multitude of your sins. When you have occasion to reprove anyone, first reprove yourself and then give your reprimand, which will be, according to circumstances, either gentle or severe. But whichever it may be, let it come from a heart which is gentle, humble and benevolent. Let your rebuke be actuated by that charity which conquers evil by good; for remember that evil cannot correct evil, and that one demon will never drive out another.

Let prayer be your most delightful recreation. Whilst you are occupying yourself with the needs of others forget yourself; but find yourself again in the secret place of your soul in holy recollection at least twice a day, in the morning and in the evening. Then put all exterior occupations on one side; raise your mind and heart to God, recommend to him all your preoccupations, and beg of him the grace to suffer in him and for him all the trials, distastes and cares of your office. Ensure that this interior prayer becomes a time of rest in weariness, so that this short hour consecrated to God alone may enable you to bear all the trials and difficulties of the day. Perfection does not consist in consolation, but rather in the submission of the will to God alone; submission above all in things that are hard and bitter. . . . Farewell.

CHAPTER XIV

THE JOURNEYS

In 1343 Friar Henry's second term of office as prior came to an end, and he took up again the life which he was to continue until his death, that of travelling up and down the country preaching. Seedtime was over and harvest had begun. Our friar met with difficulties and adventures, it is true—such were inevitable to a man of his temperament; but we read no more of failure piled on failure, for in God's scheme these were no longer necessary. As his work progressed it became more and more concerned with the great mystical movement of the Friends of God, but to the end he toiled for the salvation of sinners. In 1343 he was transferred from the priory of Constance to that of Ulm, but this meant little or no change in his mode of life.

The two great areas through which he journeyed and preached appear to have been the populous country of the Rhine basin, and the Province of Zürich lying over the Swiss border. The waterway of the Rhine, from the very earliest times, had gathered on its banks towns, some for the purposes of trade and some as fortified places to protect this trade. The Romans too had utilised the natural barrier in protecting Gaul from the inroads of the barbarians.

There was Mainz, the most ancient city on the Rhine. When Henry prayed there its cathedral had already been standing for a hundred years, the seventh to be built on that site, for the others had all been destroyed by fire. The famous minnesinger, Henry von Meissen, not twenty years dead, had been buried there.

As the friar made his way further down stream, he passed the newly built bridge of the Nahe, with low-gabled houses on either side its length instead of walls. Could this have been the place where his kinsfolk threatened to drown the woman who had fathered her bastard child on the friar?

A little farther on, at the summit of a steep hill, stood the convent of Ruprechtsberg, from the enclosure of which Saint Hildegarde, two hundred years before, had thundered forth her threats and warnings. At the Premonstratensian Abbey of Saint Margaret they were beginning to add the new apse and transept to the old church where Ludwig III had been buried in 1185.

At Renze, in 1338, during our friar's second term of priorship, a diet was held by Archbishop Baldwin of Coblenz, at which Lewis of Bavaria met Edward III of England. The latter had come on a mission, which proved abortive, to solicit Lewis's help against Philip the Fair of France. He lodged during his stay at the convent of Niederworth. This convent was built on an island in the Rhine, but two others on the mainland were so close that each one of them could hear the others chanting divine office.

When Henry went as a student to Cologne twenty-two years before, the choir of the cathedral had not long been consecrated. Now as he neared the city he could hear the chime, for by 1347 the south tower had been raised high enough to take the bells.

Between the rivers Röhr and Sieg he came into the country of his own kinsfolk, the Counts of Berg. They were all-powerful both there and at Cleves, and that perhaps was one reason why the humble friar took his mother's surname, which was not so well known in the districts through which he preached.

If the Rhine basin was famous for the history which had been made there, the history of Zürich was in the making, looking to the future. One by one the Swiss cantons were breaking away from Swabia and establishing a league of free mountain cantons. In 1335 the town of Zürich, together with the countryside dependent on it, joined the League of Uri, Schwitz and Lucerne, cutting its fortunes loose from those of Germany to throw in its lot with the growing Swiss republic.

Travelling was by no means safe in those times even for a poor mendicant friar. All along the Rhine the towns were leagued to prevent the depredations of the robber knights, only too often the stewards of archbishops or the lay nobility who owned the land. In Zürich there was political unrest, and lawlessness thrives in such soil. So Friar Henry met with more than one adventure and the perils of the way were not made any lighter for him by his natural timidity and vivid imagination.

Here are two stories, neither of them without a humorous aspect; in one of them it even appears as if a practical joke had been played on the preacher.

On returning from a preaching tour in the Netherlands, Henry and his companion made their way, as was natural, along the course of the Rhine. Henry was both ill and tired while his companion was young and active. So it happened one day that the young man, weary of accommodating his pace to the halting gait of his senior, pushed ahead, leaving the elder man to follow at his own rate; Henry may even have sent him, telling him to wait for him farther on.

The younger man went farther than Henry had intended, so the latter found himself presently alone on the outskirts of the forest, which at this place came right to the river bank. The friar was dismayed at finding no socius waiting for him, since the place had a very bad name and more than one traveller had been robbed and murdered there quite recently. It was gloomy too, for the bright sunlight on the river made the shadows on the bank look blacker and more sinister by contrast. So, his ever-ready imagination getting to work, Henry grew so nervous that he determined to wait for a while in the hope that some other traveller might appear to share the discomforts of the way.

He was just making up his mind to wait no longer but to go on alone when he heard the sound of rapidly approaching footsteps. One—no, two—travellers coming in his direction. He looked up in relief and expectation. Then his heart sank, for the young, good-looking woman who led the way was followed by a most villainous-looking ruffian, armed too with a spear and a great knife. His most unprepossessing appearance was not improved by the black jerkin he was wearing; and by the time the pair had reached the friar, Henry had fully made up his mind that his new travelling companion was undoubtedly a murderer. He looked and listened, but no one else was within sight or hearing. He could wait no longer though he was frankly terrified of these two. According to his custom in his trouble he began to pray:

"O Lord, what kind of people are these? How am I to go with them through this forest, and how will it fare with me on the journey?"

Then, making the sign of the cross, he rose to his feet and started off in front of the pair. Cold shudders crept down his spine as he heard them advancing, but he preferred the couple behind him where, if need be, he could at least make a run for it. He had not gone far when he heard the woman's pace quicken, so he put his best foot forward. But her youth and activity easily outstripped him at his best, and in a very few minutes she had caught him up, so there was nothing for it but for him to put as good a face as he could on the matter.

"What is your name, and where do you come from?" she began abruptly.

Henry told her, and when she heard that he was Henry Suso of the Friars Preachers, she cried aloud with joy.

"I have heard a great deal about you," she said, "so I will tell you about myself. The man who is following us is a robber and murderer, who makes a livelihood by robbing and murdering people in this very forest. I was born of respectable folk not far from here, but I have made a fool of myself. You mightn't think it to look at him, but that man can make himself most attractive. He deceived me, ruined me, and then carried me off by force. What else can I do but live with him?"

The woman turned abruptly and rejoined the man, to whom she began to speak in an undertone; leaving the unfortunate friar, his worst fears realised, wondering what he could do. It was characteristic that it never entered his head to console himself with the thought that a mendicant friar was hardly worth the trouble of robbing; moreover, most men of the stamp of the one behind him, being superstitious, would not risk the ill luck of killing a priest.

The babble of voices continued for a few moments, and then the man giving a great shout of laughter hurried on in his turn.

"My woman has just been telling me who you are," he said. "Now, this gives me an opportunity of easing my mind to someone who ought to be able to help me. So listen to what I am going to tell you." With that he plunged into a wild, blood-curdling tale, his eyes glancing sideways at his companion as he talked. When he saw that his stories were working, as he hoped, on the fears of the friar, he followed one up by another, each more dreadful than the last, his lips twitching a little under his black beard. As murders and robberies followed in quick succession, Henry involuntarily glanced from time to time in the direction of the river, for it was very deep and swift and he was on the outer side of the path. The robber, noticing this, suddenly stopped dead on his tracks.

"Some time ago," he began, "I was coming down this very path in company with a holy priest such as your reverence might be. Every now and then a desire to tell of my robberies and murders comes over me and I cannot rest until I have eased my mind. Afterwards?—well, I mostly repent my length of tongue and make sure that my stories go no farther. On this day, then, I was easing my mind, exactly as I am doing to-day. Then, just as I came to this spot—that's the very tree yonder—I turned on the priest, like this, drew my knife so, thrust it into his body, right up to the hilt, and then tipped him into the river, just here where the current is strong and the water deep."

"And that, O God, will be my fate also," thought Henry, as he stood his eyes glaring, fascinated by the glint of the swiftly moving knife, a cold sweat pricking out all over his body. His lips moved in a last act of contrition, then he stiffened himself and waited for the fatal blow.

But as he stood there rigid waiting, suddenly forest, trees, path and the grinning face before him began to flicker and grow dim. The next moment he felt a hand under his elbow, and he was guided to a fallen tree-trunk.

"Give over," said the woman's voice in his ears, "this is past a joke. Give no heed to his chatter, good sir, for indeed he intends you no harm."

"Take my arm," said the man; and Henry daring to do no other, rose from the tree trunk and put his hand in the other's arm. "Hark 'ee, sir, this is not the first time I have heard of you, and I have heard naught but good. Because of this I intend you no harm. Pray to God for me, that I—a poor sinner—may for your sake find mercy when I come to die."

By this time they had reached the end of the wood, and there, seated by the roadside waiting for him, was Henry's companion. The man and his woman passed on and Henry, calling his companion, sank on the ground, and there he lay more dead than alive, unable to rise for the trembling which had seized his limbs. It never entered his mind that in all probability the man's story was no more than a rough joke.

He began at once to pray for the soul of this sinner, and continued doing so for many days and weeks, until at last he received so strong an inward assurance that his prayer had been heard that he could not doubt that the poor sinner had died repentant and had gained eternal salvation.

In 1347 there was an outbreak of plague in the Rhineland; the Black Death which was devastating Europe. The Rhenish folk did not, of course, attribute this visitation to their own disregard of the most elementary laws of hygiene; someone had done them a mischief, they concluded and, looking round for a scapegrace, they fixed on the usual whipping-boy of the Middle Ages, deciding that the Jews had been poisoning the wells. Therefore they were on the look-out for any opportunity of revenge.

Just at this time Friar Henry received orders to start out on one of his preaching missions, this time to some place where he was not well known; in addition, he was given business to transact with some friends of the priory. He had to have a socius and the prior was short of men to send with him, and so, partly for want of a better, partly perhaps to give the friars at home a respite, he gave Henry as companion a lay-brother who was decidedly weak in the head and just as headstrong and obstinate as such folk often are. Henry was such a patient man, thought the prior, that he would put up with his whimsies and bear with the poor fellow, humouring him as no one else would.

So the prior sent for Henry and gave him his obedience; an obedience which filled our friar with dismay. He knew his proposed companion only too well, and he foresaw a whole series of difficulties in consequence. There was also his own unfortunate faculty for attracting trouble, so between them it would be little short of a miracle if all sorts of awkward situations did not arise. However, his business was simply to obey. The prior knew both of them, and the rest was in the hands of God.

For a while all went well, almost too well, until it chanced that early one morning the business on which Henry was engaged brought him to a village where preparations for the annual fair were in full swing. It had been raining all the previous night and both brothers were very wet. Henry wished to transact his business at once, before the opening of the fair made this impossible, but his companion suddenly turned obstinate and flatly refused to go any further until they had dried their habits and breakfasted.

Just at this moment they passed the open door of an inn through which a good fire shone warm and inviting. There the brother turned in, declaring that nothing would induce him to go any further; Henry might, of course, do as he chose, but if he went he would have to go alone. Knowing from past experience how obstinate the brother could be when this sort of mood possessed him, Henry was reluctantly obliged to leave his companion seated among a motley crowd by the inn fire, while he went in search of the person with whom he had business.

This was exactly the opportunity for which the brother had always been waiting. He was sure that he would shine if only people did not keep him so persistently in the background. So, as soon as Henry's back was turned he walked to the table and seated himself among the crowd of rough fellows—dealers, chapmen, mountebanks and the like—who were already at breakfast. There was wine, of course, potent country stuff, which soon robbed the poor brother of the few wits with which nature had endowed him, leaving him an easy prey to the roughs with whom he sat.

His meal ended, he went to the door and stood leaning against the post, gaping at the bustle going on in the courtyard outside; men unloading pack horses and preparing to set up their booths in the street. The fellows at the table winked at one another, the business of the day had not yet begun and time hung heavy on their hands. Their late breakfast companion was just the one with whom they might amuse themselves.

"Hi, you!" called out one, "you've taken a cheese of mine."

The brother's jaw dropped and his eyes opened wide; whatever were these men talking about? Said a second fellow leering at him:

"Trust a friar to lay his hand on something worth while."

"Indeed, I've taken no cheese, neither yours nor anyone else's," stammered the poor bewildered simpleton.

"Don't attempt to deny it, I saw you myself," added a third.

"You slipped your hand in his bag when Jan's face was hidden in his tankard just now," said someone from the back. Just at this moment three or four soldiers strolled up. They could see that there was some game forward and, having nothing better to do at the moment, came to join in the fun.

"Cheese?" said one. "He has more on his conscience than a paltry cheese. He's a poisoner, no less. We know him well."

At these words a great outcry arose from the bystanders, for the plague had only just abated and they were all busy looking for the Jews who were supposed to be poisoning the wells. They rushed forward and made the lay-brother prisoner.

For a moment he was near fainting with terror; and then with that cunning instinct of self-preservation so often found in the witless, he suddenly saw a way out of the dilemma. He had no mind to be put in the village gaol or ducked in the river.

"You are making a mistake, friends," he cried out. "I am not the poisoner; you can see for yourselves the poor witless fool that I be. I've not the mind to plan such a thing even if I were wishful to. If you want the real poisoner, then go seek my companion, for he is a learned man and deep in the councils of the Order. He has been sent here by our superior to poison all the wells even as far as Alsace. You see how he has left me here, and slipped off to poison your own well in this very village. If you drink from it, by night you will be dead every mother's son of you. For my part, this business is great grief and shame to me, and I have refused to have anything to do with it, and that is the reason why he has gone off alone and left me behind. If you want proof of the truth

101

of my words, only look at his great bag. It looks innocent enough, just as if it were used to carry his books. But if you were to open it, you would find it filled to the brim with little packets of deadly poison, and the florins that the Jews have given him for carrying out their wicked work. If you doubt me, open his bag and see for yourselves."

It only needed the mention of the Jews to convince the crowd of the truth of what the brother was saying; for it was just the thing that they wanted to believe. So, seizing one a sword, another a pike, and another some farm implement, they rushed off down the street, shouting as they ran: "Where is the poisoner? Where is the wicked murderer? Let us find and kill him." And not finding the friar, they rushed into all the houses in the street, pulling open the closet doors, and thrusting their naked swords into the straw mattresses, shouting and raging until the whole fair rang with the uproar, and the countryfolk left the business of buying and selling to join in the chase.

Of course, among those gathered for the fair there were reputable men who knew the friar. These did their best to reassure the mob, telling them that Friar Henry was well known for his learning and piety, the last man in the world to go about poisoning wells. But the crowd would have none of it. "You'd best be quiet," they were told, "or you'll have us believe that you're tarred with the same brush and so deserve a ducking with the pestilent friar." After that everyone held his tongue in fear.

Meanwhile Henry, in blissful ignorance of what had happened in his absence, made his way to the inn, for his business was completed, and he thought that his companion would have dried his clothes and breakfasted, and be in a more reasonable mood in consequence. He found the place in a turmoil, the lay-brother gone, and mine host with a long face and a tale of some sort of dispute which had ended in the brother's being locked up by the burgomaster.

Henry said nothing but inwardly he groaned. He might

have guessed what would happen if he left the brother alone. But then, what else could he have done? The business was urgent and he could not drag his companion with him by main force. There was nothing for it now but to go to the burgomaster's house and see what could be done in the matter.

For a long time he could do absolutely nothing. The lawyer would not hear of releasing the brother. Even if he were not responsible for his actions, as the friar pleaded, he had managed to stir up a perfectly disgraceful riot, and on this day too of all days. Their fair day would be a byword in the villages round for a twelve-month. In any case, if he were the simpleton Henry pretended, why had his prior sent him travelling, and why had the friar left him to himself? No, the best place for him was the watch-tower dungeon, and there he was going. Henry argued and pleaded, but for a long time without success. At last, however, more to be rid of his importunity than for any other reason, the burgomaster gave in, and Henry, after paying a large fine, was free to take the lay-brother away with him.

It was about the hour of vespers when the two left the burgomaster's house, and they had not gone far when they suddenly came face to face with a part of the mob, who were on the point of giving up the fruitless search. The instant they espied the two religious the thrill of the hunt was renewed and with a yell they rushed on Henry, shouting that at last the poisoner was found; the friar turned back, but a second crowd, hearing the cries, began to close in from behind, and in less than a minute he found himself surrounded by a mob of angry men all yelling:

"Here's the poisoner; here's that devil! What shall we do?"

There ensued perfect pandemonium as every man of them began to shout suggestions as to the best way of making an end of him. Some were all for drowning him in the Rhine; while others, declaring that his evil carcase would pollute the water, wished to burn him. Then one huge lubberly fellow in a sooty jerkin, seizing a pike, pushed himself to the front of the crowd and shouted to the rest:

"Hear me, good masters, this heretic deserves to die a shameful death. So say I. Therefore, let me spit him through on this pike, and then drive it into yonder fence, and let him hang there like a toad or rat that he is, for all the world to see. Let's leave his carcase here to be cursed by every passer-by. Then he will reap the punishment he so richly deserves, both in this world and the next."

This suggestion was received with acclamation, and a dispute at once arose as to who was to have the honour of doing the deed. There were friends of the friar's in the crowd; there were others also who had no desire for this summary vengeance. Between them, taking advantage of the dispute, they seized the friar, pushed and shuffled him back between them until he reached the outskirts of the crowd, then they hustled him off, bidding him hurry away to a neighbouring village where he might find shelter.

Henry hurried off alone, for at the first sound of renewed disturbance his companion had disappeared. But the villagers had heard of the trouble and, having no mind to be dragged out of their beds by the mob, refused to take the friar in. Some of the women would indeed have done so if they had not been scared of harm for their children.

Too weary to go farther, Henry crept into the hedge which bordered a garden. It was a thorny bed, but he was hidden and the pain of his scratched face and hands seemed somehow in keeping with the rest. Then he began to pray:

"O Father of all pity, when wilt thou bring help to me in my great need? O God of kindness, hast thou forgotten thy kindness to me? O Father, good Father, help me in these straits. To thee I commend my soul."

A priest who was passing, and who knew of the tumult with which the excited populace were renewing their search, heard the friar praying in the thicket and, calling to

Der selig hainrich sus ze coßtentz geborn am bodiner see
Nam die ewig wysshait zům gmahel gaißtlicher ee
Sein gespons tet in den namen verwanndett
Amandus hieß sy in nennen in allen launden
Sein leben wz er in irm dienst verzeret   crē
Des fröd sich vlm die sein grab vnd hailtů halt in

"AMANDUS"

From an early engraving

him, took him privily away to his own house where he kept him for the night. Next morning, with the first light of day, the priest sent him again on his journey. And so Friar Henry, for this time, saw an end of his troubles.

CHAPTER XV

THE MYSTICS

GERMANY has always been a home of speculative mysticism. In the fourteenth century the Rhineland, Henry Suso's country, was the centre of several schools of mystic thought; there were the orthodox and the heretical beguines and beghards, the Brethren of the Free Spirit, and the Friends of God.

Throughout the whole Rhine country were to be found these free associations of pious men and women, called beguines and beghards. Some lived alone, but generally they were united in great beguinages in which, as a rule, each beguine or beghard had a separate house, where they lived a kind of eremetical life. These communities were governed either by a superior of their own or by an ecclesiastic from outside; they took the three vows of religion but only for the duration of their sojourn in the beguinage which they were free to leave. It is easy to understand how many of these recluses, studying the secrets of mystical theology unprotected by firm monastic discipline, fell into heresy, in general some form of Quietism. At the time of which we are speaking there were two distinct groups of beguines, the orthodox and the false. The heretical beguines had already become so numerous and so dangerous that at the Council of Vienna in 1311 the German bishops petitioned for their condemnation.

The heretical beguines were greatly influenced by another school of false mystics called the Brethren of the Free Spirit, whose chief centre of activity was at Cologne. They were a secret society who disseminated such insidious pantheistic and quietist doctrines that some even among Catholic theologians were infected by their teaching. They taught that the intellectual nature of man possessed of itself perfect beatitude, and so it had no need of the light of glory to raise it to the vision and beatific enjoyment of God. Man, said they, in his present state was capable of reaching such a degree of glory as to become impeccable, and so could no longer grow in grace. In this state, therefore, there was no need of prayer and fasting because, the senses being entirely subject to reason, the body could be allowed to satisfy all its desires. Such teaching, carried to its logical conclusion, led to all kinds of immorality.

To fight against such errors there was founded between the years 1338 and 1343 the Association of the Friends of God, having its chief centres at Basle, Strassburg and Cologne. The sole bond of union between the associates was a common desire of holiness. They aimed at sanctity for themselves and the edification of their neighbour by the practice of Catholic devotion.

The precursors of this movement were three great women mystics of the Cistercian convent of Helfta: Mechtilde of Magdeburg, Saint Mechtilde of Hackeborn, and Saint Gertrude the Great.

Mechtilde of Magdeburg, in her youth a beguine, entered Helfta late in life, bringing with her the first six books of a treatise she had written called *The Light of the Divinity*. These books, written in Low German, were collected by the Dominican, Henry of Halle. While she was at Helfta she wrote a seventh volume. The whole of them have come down to us in two volumes; one in High German from the pen of Henry of Nördlingen, the secular priest who shared with Suso and Tauler the chief direction of· the Friends of

God; the other is in Latin. They are attractive in style, couched in noble language, rich in imagery, lyrical, and embodying a very elevated mystic teaching.

Saint Mechtilde of Hackeborn wrote *A Book of Special Grace*. The subjects of which she treats are: Liturgical prayer, our last end, the Communion of Saints, and familiarity with Christ.

Saint Gertrude is the saint of our Lord's humanity; she extols the riches of the liturgy, the glory and magnificence of the Sacred Heart, the death of the elect, and purgatory. Her work is distinguished by its fullness, theological exactitude, and the splendour of her theology. It unites the wealth of the pseudo-Dionysius with the precision of Saint Thomas Aquinas.

In its early days the Association of the Friends of God was fostered chiefly by the Dominicans, for the Order of Preachers flourished exceedingly in Germany at that epoch. There were a hundred and seventy-four priories in Germany, of which seventy were in the Rhineland, and seven in Strassburg alone. The fourteenth century was pre-eminently the century of Dominican spirituality; prayerful because of its choral use of the liturgy; austere because of its teaching of the intrinsic efficacy of grace; and speculative because it is the Order of Truth.

The father of the Friends of God was Master Eckhart of Cologne. No great quantity of his writings has come down to us, but from the first there was controversy about some of his expressions, both written and spoken, which were capable of a quietistic interpretation. Before his death he publicly retracted anything which could be understood as in any way contrary to the teaching of the Church, but his name has remained under a cloud and it was left to his spiritual followers and sons, especially Suso and Tauler, to give an entirely orthodox interpretation of his mystical teaching.

Tauler was born in Strassburg about 1290 and joined the

Preachers in 1308. He was one of the most famous preachers of his time and was called the "sublime" and "illuminated" doctor. The only authentic work of his which we have is a volume of eighty-three sermons. His teaching followed Saint Denis, Saint Thomas Aquinas and Eckhart; to the mystical teaching of the last he gave an orthodox interpretation. He preached to the beguines and his own Dominican nuns, teaching resignation, renunciation of self, love of solitude and high mysticism. Both he and Suso had almost innumerable disciples among laymen and priests, also religious, both men and women.

There was the Dominican Convent at Engelthal where lived Christine Ebner and her cousin, Adelaide Langmann, both of whom have left books of spiritual instruction. At the convent of Maria Medingen, between Nuremburg and Augsburg, lived their cousin Marguerite Ebner, the spiritual daughter of Henry of Nördlingen. Then there were the convents of Adelhausen, Unterlinden, Diessenhofen, Töss and Ottenbach.

Best known among the lay Friends of God was Rulman Merswin, a citizen of Strassburg. He wrote forty-two treatises in German, purporting to be the work of the "Great Friend of God of the Oberland." The most famous of these, *The Master's Book*, tells how he converted a Master of Sacred Scripture, long identified with Tauler. The mysterious "Friend of God" was reputed to be either Nicholas of Basle, burnt by the Inquisition in 1397, or the hermit, John of Coire. It is now generally admitted that the whole was an invention of Merswin himself, who wrote a series of mystic romances. Another Friend of God was Henry of Langenstein, a mathematician, astronomer, theologian, and philosopher of the school of Ockam, who wrote two excellent treatises on *Contempt of the World*, and *The Mirror of the Soul*.

A brief summary of German mysticism as taught by the Friends of God will not be out of place here. It was in general speculative and intellectualistic; it was abstract; and, except in the case of Suso, it remained enclosed within the soul, and made no attempt to arrive at the contemplation of God through the contemplation of his creation. Lastly it offered its appeal to all. Tauler, for instance, taught through sermons for the liturgical seasons, sermons which were intended for the mass of the faithful as much as for his religious children.

It may be epitomised in these three points: total renunciation of self, and absolute submission to the divine will, in preparation for union with God; complete stripping of the intellect of all intellectual and sensible images; mystic union itself which operated through a species of return of the soul to the divine unity.

Self-renunciation and resignation to the divine will, inspired by the gift of fortitude and counsel, must dominate the whole of life. Everyone must rest content with the vocation to which God has called him, for God is the Master who may do what he pleases. Every happening must be accepted with entire resignation for all are directed by God for his glory and our salvation. In order that a man should hold himself ready to be stripped of everything, he must submit with resignation and patience to the loss of honour and reputation.

This interior mortification is far more painful than any bodily austerity; but, as it is necessary for the death of self-love, it is indispensable for all those who wish to reach a high degree of sanctity. Furthermore, the man who desires perfection must renounce also all spiritual consolation. Our Lord may will that he should endure abandonment both by God and by his fellow men, that he should experience doubt and sadness, that he should even, perhaps, be tempted to despair. He must accept this patiently since it is God's will.

He will accept this trial in union with Christ who ordained that during his sacred Passion he should suffer the grief of apparent abandonment by his Father. These German mystics are perhaps the first to speak of the grief of the soul of Christ when he seemed to be abandoned by God. One of the most painful sufferings of the loving soul is when it finds itself apparently abandoned by God. What an insight is given, then, to the lives of these mystics who have placed in such high relief this aspect of the Passion, the abandonment which forced from the lips of the dying Christ the cry: " My God, my God, why hast thou forsaken me?"

The final renunciation is that of the will. Self-will dies when every action is performed for the love of God, with no return on self but solely to glorify our Lord. The will is empty of self, since it desires nothing but God's will. When the soul rests in its own nothingness there is made within it such a silence as to render it capable of receiving God within it and hearing his voice.

In mystic union the will of a man identifies itself with the will of God, which identification must be prepared for by prolonged exercises in more and more complete submission to the divine will. The intellect must also be prepared by being stripped of all images. Images are the sensible, imaginative representations of an object; intelligible species are the abstract forms of these objects which become ideas. To reach contemplation the mind must rid itself of images and species, raising itself above the intellect and imagination to unite itself closely to God. But the soul must have arrived at a certain degree of perfection first; for it is harmful to desire to unite the soul to God too soon by an act of understanding freed from all acts of the imagination. Meditation on our Lord's life and passion is useful and sanctifying, and no one who does not make use for a long time of such considerations can arrive at sanctity. But a moment comes when such images make but little impression and the soul desires ardently to be united to the divine nature. Then it must turn from all images, for its thought will be occupied by the divine essence and the Trinity.

Since it is impossible for us to know God by means of

images, for he utterly surpasses all our conceptions, we must know him in a negative manner. If the intellect is stripped of itself it receives the brilliance and splendour of the divine light which takes the place of the light of reason. The soul reaches the divine darkness where all forms and images are silent; and this supernatural silence, where all is calm and in peace, shares even in the knowledge of God.

According to Tauler we are all called and invited to this intimate union of the soul with God, and so he teaches all the faithful how to prepare for it. He declares it to be inexpressible, for knowledge alone will never attain it. It fills the heart with a great jojy; the beatitude to which the contemplative state leads is a participation, in a passing manner appropriate to our present condition, in the celestial happiness.

Following the pseudo-Dionysius the German mystics hold that we come from God and we return to him; we come from him by creation and we return to him by contemplation. All created beings have existed eternally in the divine essence as in their exemplar. They have always been present in the thought of God, as in the archetype and model according to which they were created. Inasmuch as they were conformed to the divine idea; all beings before creation were one thing with the essence of God, just as ideas are one and the same thing with the intelligence which conceives them.

All creatures, then, were one with God. From this unity multiplicity has come forth. God, in time, has created different beings conformable to the image which was in him. They come, then, from him, not as an emanation of his substance, but because they have been created according to the eternal exemplar.

Man has been created according to the eternal image in God. The German mystics teach that this image rests in the superior part of the soul, and that thus we resemble God and the Blessed Trinity.

The image resting in us has something of divinity. It is the divine image according to which we were created. We are not, however, for this reason transformed into the divine being, because the soul always remains distinct from God. This divine likeness exists in all men, but often it is hidden beneath sin and imperfections. The work of the spiritual life consists in freeing the soul that we may be united to God. By the practice of virtue, above all of renunciation, the soul reaches that stripping of the intellect which is necessary to free it for contemplation.

As the soul comes from God it must return to him. This return will take place in heaven. Here below it has its beginnings only in mystic union. The mystic union which constitutes this return to the divine unity has three characteristics: it operates in the essence of the soul and not in its faculties; it permits of no intermediary between the soul and God; in some fashion it removes the difference which exists between the soul and God. It is unity without difference, and for that reason it is unity.

The whole subject of mystic union, according to the Friends of God, is fraught with difficulties, and much of what they say is very obscure, so it is safer to turn to Suso himself, on whose writings the Church has set her seal, in order to obtain some further ideas of the subject.

CHAPTER XVI

THE TEACHING

MYSTICAL life is the full development of a perfect Christian life. In its broadest application it is the union of the soul with God through faith in charity. In order to attain eminent sanctity this union must be consummated; that is, it must bring forth fruit in love of the souls for whom Christ died. So far this ideal is the common possession of all Christians; but, as "star differeth from star in glory," and as "in my Father's house there are many mansions," so there are no two saints who reach sanctity in precisely the same way. The period in which each lives, the country to which he belongs, his own personal make-up—each plays a part in moulding his own peculiar type of holiness.

To Suso belonged a mystical life which corresponded to the needs of Germany in the fourteenth century; it was also a type which is impressed on the Friars Preachers, the family likeness to their great Father, Saint Dominic; but it was also something incommunicable of his own, a mysticism which corresponded to his own temperament, his surroundings; to all that, in fact, which differentiates Suso from every other saint, every other Dominican, every other German of the fourteenth century.

If we wish to learn in what Blessed Henry's mysticism consists, there is no surer teacher than himself as he reveals himself in his writings. These first are extracts from a series of instructions, given to a nun, on union with God:

The interior life consists in complete renunciation, and death to self in God.

A man who would truly renounce himself in God must carefully carry out these four rules. His conduct should be straightforward, serious and prudent. His good actions should be the natural result of his interior dispositions. He will preserve his sensitive nature in peace and will not dissipate recollection in seeking for news; for a man who is greedy of knowledge, and is for ever gossiping about what this one says and that one does, is always distracted by illusions and earthly images, and is incapable of enjoying interior peace where vain phantoms cannot disturb his repose. The man who has truly renounced himself will not crave for any created thing, because he is convinced that all which is outside God is mere emptiness and nothingness. He will never dispute with nor speak against anyone, but will be full of love for everyone, especially those whom God uses to detach him from himself.

Let him who desires peace love with an equal love both success and adversity. Let him rest equally united to God in gain and in loss. If you truly desire to renounce your life in Christ abandon all your own possessions, whether material or intellectual; go out of yourself that you may hide yourself in God. In whatsoever way he may treat you, either himself or through the agency of his creatures, in adversity or in prosperity, be always and in all things submissive to God.

Close your senses to all images and forms of creatures; live free and disengaged from all that reason usually chooses under the influence of self-love, self-will, sensuality and desire of pleasure. Do not allow yourself to be disturbed by anything outside God. Here, in a few words, you may learn through what degrees the soul should return to union with the God who created her.

First, the soul must purify herself from all vice and separate herself generously from all the pleasures of the world to attach herself to God by continual prayer, by isolation from all creatures, and by holy exercises which subject, without cessation, the flesh to the spirit. She ought to offer herself willingly and courageously to the numberless trials and sorrows which come to her either from God directly, or through the medium of creatures. She must then impress on her heart the Passion of Christ crucified; she must engrave on her spirit the sweetness of his evangelical precepts, his profound humility, the purity of his life. She must do this in order to love and imitate him, because it is only in the company of Jesus that she can go still farther and reach the unitive life. To enter into this life, all exterior preoccupations must be sacrificed, the soul must enclose herself in the silent peace of the spirit, must so resign herself to God in all things as to be completely and for ever dead to her own self and self-will. She must love above all things the honour and glory of Christ and his Father, and must bear the greatest affection to all men, both friends and foes.

Let the man who is actively preoccupied by the movements of his exterior senses cease these operations to apply himself to the interior exercise of simple contemplation. Then the soul, little by little, will reach abandonment of the natural use of her faculties of understanding and will. She then begins to realise interiorly a supernatural and divine assurance which will lead her to higher perfection. She will be freed from all self-love and all natural activity of intellect and will. In this perfect state the soul will be delivered from the weight of her imperfections, and will lift herself by divine grace to a place of interior light where she will taste without intermission the abundance of heavenly consolations, and where she will learn to know with wisdom and execute with prudence all that God and right reason ask of her. In this state the spirit is ravished beyond time and space in sweet and loving contemplation of God.

But this is not the highest degree of perfection, because the soul still distinguishes herself and her own actions from God, and she knows creatures in their particular nature. He who detaches himself still more from himself, and penetrates more intimately into God, experiences a divine ravishment, not through his own power, but by a superior grace which draws his created spirit into the uncreated Spirit of God, and there it is made to taste of that ecstasy experienced by Saint Paul of which Saint Bernard and other saints speak.

In this state the soul no longer knows form, images, multiplicity; she finds herself in forgetfulness and ignorance of self and all creatures because she sees, knows, and is conscious of God only. There, without effort, without application, drawn by God alone and made one with him by grace, she raises herself above herself and becomes absorbed and buried in the abyss of the divinity where she experiences all the joys of beatitude.

This is what he writes to one of his friends concerning the purification, the illumination and the perfection of a holy soul:

My dear friend,

God has not called his servants to a mediocre, ordinary life, but rather to the perfection of a sublime holiness since he said to his disciples: "Be ye perfect as your heavenly Father is perfect." In heaven the inferior angels are purified, enlightened, and rendered perfect by the superior angels; such is the doctrine of Denis the Areopagite. This is brought to pass by the splendour which shines from the eternal Son, the principle of essences, through the communication of new aspirations and truths. What is accomplished in heaven also takes place on earth in regard to the servants of God, who are also purified and enlightened and sanctified. Purification consists in banishing from the mind all created images, even to that of the highest apostle, the highest seraph. Man must die to all created things and allow no image, no creature-form, to enter the soul, which should be free to think of its Creator only.

After purgation—the emptying of the soul—comes the illumination and brightness of divine light; for the Word is a light to illumine the darkness of ignorance. This light often reaches the soul without intermediary, and in this it always experiences joy and well-being, since the light brings with it divine forms and images. The more vivifying and abundant it is the more perfectly a man dies to the vain, perishable things of earth, to clothe himself in incorruption. Temporal things become distasteful to him and he cannot occupy himself with them without weariness and disgust.

From this illumination comes the perfection of the soul. It consists in the complete union of our powers and intellectual faculties with God. We unite ourselves to him by sublime contemplation, ardent love and delightful enjoyment of the sovereign good, in so far as the weakness of our nature permits. But since the soul joined to a frail body can never unite itself so intimately to the pure and sovereign good as the greatness and sublimity of such an alliance demands, it must choose certain holy and divine images which are able to draw it away from itself and raise it to God. Among such images the first is the image and example of Jesus Christ, God and man, the maker of all the saints, in whom is found life itself, the reward and happiness of the soul. He who transforms himself into the image of Christ Jesus reaches contemplation of the glory of the Lord. Borne up by the Holy Spirit, the soul goes beyond the light of the most holy humanity to transform itself in the brightness of his eternal divinity. So, my dear friend, the more we fix our eyes on the sacred humanity of Jesus, and the more we conform ourselves to his life, the more we shall rejoice in God and the greater will be our happiness in heaven.

In the *Little Book of Eternal Wisdom* Suso tells us in what true renunciation consists and how the soul becomes one thing with God:

DISCIPLE: Tell me, Eternal Wisdom, how your servants suffer and die who while they are on earth renounce themselves in God. I am sure that they lead a most pure life, always tending to that which is most perfect.

ETERNAL WISDOM: A man can only renounce himself in God by the complete observance of the law and by the greatest purity of heart; because he who loves creatures and himself has not the purity of my love and can never renounce his own will. But my servants live always in the most perfect way, detached from themselves both within and without, and free from all ownership in body or in soul. In trials they are so strong and constant that they despise suffering, which they count as nothing. They are so prepared for death that not only do they receive it with submission from the hand of God, but they love it, they desire it more than any earthly treasure and they do not desire to live a moment unless in the fulfilment of my will.

DISCIPLE: In order to walk in the perfect way of renunciation, which is the more necessary, contemplation or action?

ETERNAL WISDOM: These two things ought not to be separated; to what purpose is it for men to seek virtue, union with God and renunciation if they do not conquer their own natures; if in subduing their passions and practising virtue they are not set free from sin? In this case the more a man studies the deeper will he fall, because he prides himself on his knowledge, because he keeps no guard on himself and so obtains a false liberty which captivates and ruins him.

DISCIPLE: That is the abuse of knowledge, and it is not surprising that so many clever men are lost. But a man cannot abuse austerity of life and the rigours of holy penance.

ETERNAL WISDOM: This is only true if the interior corresponds to the exterior; for there are people who are very mortified exteriorly but they have not renounced themselves in God.

DISCIPLE: Nevertheless, suffering is imitation of Christ and the Cross.

ETERNAL WISDOM: It would be more true to call it an appearance of imitation of the Cross. These people do not wish to conform their lives to that of Jesus Christ, which was gentleness and humility itself. They judge and blame their neighbour only too easily. They despise and condemn all who do not live as they do; and if one wishes to know them as they really are, one has only to wound them in their self-will and the good opinion they have of themselves. Then they are found to be full of pride and disquietude. It is very evident that they do not possess Christian renunciation nor have they ever learnt how to abandon themselves to God in reality. They have died neither to themselves nor to their own wills. Under the appearance of an austere life they have preserved the full strength of their passions, they have fed and made their own wills strong.

DISCIPLE: Whence comes the true interior and exterior renunciation of the elect in perfect unity with God?

ETERNAL WISDOM: From generation and sonship in God; all my

true servants are sons of God, as it is said in St. John: "He gives them the power to become the sons of God, who are born of God," so they participate through grace in the nature and act of God; for the Father always begets one like to himself in nature and in action. The just who renounce themselves in God, by this union which is eternal, triumph in time and possess a blessed life which transforms them in God.

DISCIPLE: But I do not understand how so many creatures have in God only one existence; for there is infinity between the just and God, between the Creator and his creatures.

ETERNAL WISDOM: My son, if you reason according to the senses, and if you desire to reach eternal truth through natural knowledge, you will never be capable of understanding what you ask me. Time and eternity are one and the same thing in God; and the temporal being of the creature in the nature and essence of God has no longer any diversity. Raise yourself above your senses and you will understand what you desire.

The disciple was ravished out of himself and lived for twelve weeks in ecstasy. He no longer knew if he was in the world or out of it, because in this vision, he only understood and realised a God who was unique and simple, without distinguishing the multitude and variety of creatures. When the vision was ended, the Eternal Wisdom said to him:

ETERNAL WISDOM: What has happened, my friend? Where are you and what have you understood? Have I not spoken the truth to you?

DISCIPLE: Yes, Lord, it is certain that I could never have understood so well if I had not experienced it. I think that I now understand the end and aim of the lives of your friends who have perfectly renounced themselves in you. The senses recognise many distinct things and the mind sees in God no difference.

ETERNAL WISDOM: That is true, because the soul through the way of perfect renunciation can lose itself in God to its infinite advantage. It can bury itself in the divine essence where it no longer distinguishes anything but God, when it no longer knows created forms by means of images but only in God himself.

Now you think that you understand God when you call him

118

the supreme spirit, the all-pure intelligence, essence, goodness, strength, love and happiness; but you are in reality farther from understanding God than earth is from heaven. It is only in reaching the centre of the divinity, which is the unity of all things, that a man penetrates and comprehends God without comprehending him; because such a one knows him in an incomprehensible manner and the soul no more distinguishes itself from God. But you are incapable of this marvellous change where the soul, in the abyss of the divinity, transforms herself in the unity of God to lose herself and confound herself with him, not in regard to her nature, but with regard to her life and faculties. For him who enters eternity there is no more past, no more future, only the present. For him who is transformed in the unity of God there is no more distinction; only one being, one only joy. But this grace of a perfect union, immutable and eternal, is the lot and the happiness of the blessed in heaven. You cannot quench your thirst at these springs of glory during your pilgrimage on earth; here you receive a few drops only as a foretaste of what is destined for you.

DISCIPLE: O loving Wisdom, how will a man act who is with God? Will he lose his powers and their operation?

ETERNAL WISDOM: No, when he is entirely immersed in union with God and becomes one thing with him, he does not lose his powers any more than he loses his nature; but he acts no longer as a man because he sees and grasps all in the divine unity. Philosophers consider things as dependent on their natural causes; but my servants raise themselves higher and consider them as they come from God. This consideration leads a man to God after death, provided that he has conformed himself to God's will; and in this divine change, in this supreme unity, he regards himself and all other creatures as they are in eternity.

DISCIPLE: Can a man see himself as a creature if, in eternity and in God, he is one with God? The same nature cannot be at the same time created and uncreated.

ETERNAL WISDOM: In this union a man knows that he is a creature; that when he had no existence, he was conformed to his idea or image in God, and that he was none other than God; as St. John says: "That which was made had life in him." I do not say that man was a creature in God, for God is none other than Unity and Trinity; but I say that a man who in a superior and ineffable manner is in God, becomes one and the same thing with God while still retaining his particular and natural being.

He does not lose this but he enjoys it divinely, and he lives in a perfect manner since he does not lose that which he already has and he acquires that which he has not, that is to say, a divine existence. The soul in God remains a creature; but, in this abyss of the divinity in which she loses herself, she does not consider whether she exists or whether she is a creature. She takes her life, her essence, her happiness, all that she is, in God; and being held in this way fixed and immovable in him, without seeing anything of herself, she is at peace and rests in this ocean of happiness, knowing no other essence than that which is God. When the soul has learnt to see and contemplate God, she goes forth from God in a manner of speaking, and finds herself in the natural order. It is this knowledge of God which we call *the evening knowledge* because the creature distinguishes herself in God; whilst in the *morning knowledge* she knows herself in God without image, without difference, as God is in himself.

DISCIPLE: If there is no interchange between God and the soul, how is there union?

ETERNAL WISDOM: The essence of the soul is united to the essence of God; the powers and faculties of the soul are united to the act of God; and then the soul realises that she is united to God in his infinite Being where she obtains fruition.

DISCIPLE: Can a man during his lifetime attain such union?

ETERNAL WISDOM: Yes. Not by his intellectual faculties, but by the divine uplifting, which raises his soul beyond the things of time.

DISCIPLE: Can a man sin while he is in this state?

ETERNAL WISDOM: If he returns to himself he can sin. But he does not sin while he is in this state of union. As St. John says: "He who is born of God does not sin because the seed of God is in him."

DISCIPLE: What act results from so high a state of union?

ETERNAL WISDOM: There is but one possible, because the principle of his union is unity, even as the divine essence.

DISCIPLE: Does he then lose his understanding and will?

ETERNAL WISDOM: No, but he only possesses them under the influence and act of God.

DISCIPLE: How do you explain that the soul loses herself entirely in God?

ETERNAL WISDOM: She understands and desires nothing but God; and in this union she sees nothing of created things. She does not turn back on herself; she does not reflect on her own intelligence and will; she is completely buried in the abyss of the divinity. There she holds herself in silence, she sleeps, she rests in ineffable sweetness. And then it can truly be said that she loses herself, not in respect to her nature, but in respect to the ownership of her powers, since she can then neither understand nor will one thing in preference to another; and she truly desires none other than God himself. In this consists her perfect liberty, because she neither desires nor can desire other than God; that is to say, she never desires evil but always desires good. That is why Saint Augustine says: "Take away this or that particular good, and, if you can, consider good in itself; that is the Supreme Good to which we are tending."

And the means for attaining perfection:

ETERNAL WISDOM: A man should dwell in his centre, which is God. He leaves it by the exclusive love of himself and creatures, thus usurping what belongs to the Creator. In his blindness he has snatched himself away from God, and has poured himself forth in criminal love of creatures. So, in order to return to God, he must, first of all, permeate himself in the knowledge of his own nothingness which, when separated from God and his all-powerful virtue, is absolute nothingness. Secondly, he must consider his nature brought forth and preserved in the being of God, but unhappily stained by his own malice, in order that this nature may be purified, tamed, and led back to God. Thirdly, he must raise himself by generous self-hatred, detach himself from the multiplicity of earthly loves, renounce himself, and abandon himself to God and his good pleasure in all things; in joy as in suffering, in work as in rest. This renunciation must be so complete that he will never take back his gift to God of himself, his union of spirit with Christ Jesus, which is so close that he sees and does all in him and by him, as Saint Paul says: "I live, now not I, but Christ liveth in me." In that consists the true renunciation of self in God. So abandon yourself utterly for the love of God, and in this way you will become truly happy.

CHAPTER XVII

THE NUNS

Among the Friends of God, of whom mention has just been made, was a Dominican nun of the convent of Töss, in the province of Zürich, near Winterthur. Her name was Elsbeth Stagel, or Staglin, and for many years she was directed in the spiritual life by Friar Henry. Towards the end of her life she became almost completely an invalid and, in her frequent attacks of illness, she was accustomed to turn to her old friend and father for help and comfort.

By dint of questioning she succeeded in drawing from him the story of his own spiritual life; all of which he told her in the strictest confidence. To quote Henry's own words: "As she found comfort and direction in these things, she wrote them down to be a help both to herself and to others; and this she did by stealth, so that he—the friar—knew it not. Later, when he discovered the spiritual theft, he reproved her for it and, forcing her to give the writing to him, he burnt all there was of it. But when the rest was given to him and he was about to burn that, he was stopped by a heavenly messenger from God forbidding it." This unburnt portion of manuscript was the basis of his own autobiography. But as it was probably copied out and embellished later by his good friends the nuns of Töss, the manuscript as it has come down to us—for we have not the original in his own handwriting—contains a certain element of femininity which is somewhat out of harmony with the rest.

Töss is perhaps the best-loved of all the convents which called Henry Suso father, though there are others famous in the annals of south Germany; such, for instance, as the priory of Saint Margaret at Strassburg, Unterlinden in Colmar, and Engelthal in Zürich. Elsbeth Staglin has left an account of the priory at Töss, showing its connection with the friar, and from this it is possible to generalise about the other priories of which he was the spiritual father. The priory itself has completely disappeared and factory buildings cover the site.

One night the inhabitants of the district of Winterthur saw beautiful and shining lights hanging in the air, though no one could tell what they were nor whence they had come. Near the river was a small beguinage, and people wondered at first if these lights signified the prayer of these recluses. But the nobles of the place decided that the lights were a prophecy of the future, and so they agreed to build a priory for nuns of the newly founded Dominican Order on the place over which the lights had hung.

On the place where they proposed erecting the convent stood the mill of the district, so they gave the miller notice to quit, promising at the same time to build him a new mill. The poor miller was filled with dismay, for he loved his mill and the millstream, and could not bear to think that the clatter of the wheel was to be replaced by the sound of psalmody; so he did all in his power to postpone the evil day when he must make way for builders.

It happened one night, as he stayed working late in the mill, he heard a voice calling him: "Why do you dispute my right to the place where I wish to set up my own dwelling?"

The same thing happened for three nights in succession, and since he too had seen the mysterious lights he knew that the voice could only come from heaven. Frightened lest he should withstand God, he gave up his mill at once. In 1233 Bishop Henry of Constance authorised the foundation of the priory, and granted an indulgence of forty days to all who should help in the building. In 1240 the same Bishop consecrated the church and took the priory under his own protection. In the course of the thirteenth and fourteenth centuries the renown of the place spread far and wide, and the community increased in consequence until the house maintained between sixty and a hundred religious. In 1315 the then Bishop of Constance consecrated a new church, for the community had far outgrown the limits of the old one.

The foundation at Töss was made at a time when the friars, fearing lest their numbers should prove insufficient to fulfil their office of preaching and to direct at the same time many new convents of nuns, had obtained from the Pope a decree dispensing them from the charge of the sisters of their Order. But an exception was made in the case of Töss, for Pope Innocent IV himself entrusted the care of the new priory to the Preachers of the Province of Germany. The brethren of Zürich were directed to send the nuns visitators, confessors and preachers; and from that time the brethren never failed in their spiritual aid. Among some of the famous men who held the office of preacher at Töss were Wolfwam, Provincial of Suabia; Hugh of Staufen, Lector at Constance, and their father and friend *par excellence*, Henry Suso.

Sister Elsbeth Stagel, our authority for all that concerns Töss, was born at Zürich probably at the beginning of the fourteenth century, and entered the priory at Töss when quite young. Moved by a vehement desire for perfection, she began to study all she could find about the mystical life. Straightway she plunged into the works of Eckhart—strong meat indeed for one only just emerging from spiritual infancy.

Needless to say she was soon out of her depth and, to quote Friar John of the Blessed Virgin, " she became much perplexed in soul by these elevations, interior deaths, simplifications, unions and deiform transformations, and other secrets of the mystical life which are concealed under these and the like obscure and unknown terms." Finding herself in dire need of an experienced living spiritual guide to steer her through these deep waters, she wrote to Henry, of whom she had heard as a wise and experienced director, asking him to undertake the guidance of her soul. At first Henry was not at all willing to comply, for in the first place he was astonished that anyone who had studied the wisdom of Eckhart should turn to such a poor substitute; and in the second place, he feared lest her request should be prompted by simple curiosity and a naïve desire to converse learnedly about the spiritual life, whereas "true holiness does not dwell in fine words but in good works." At last, however, won over by her gentle persistence, he agreed to direct her.

At first his direction was remarkable chiefly for its extreme prudence. He considered Sister Elsbeth very young and inexperienced, and so he told her that she must not expect God to initiate her into the mysteries of the contemplative life before she had first undergone a hard apprenticeship. She must first take the path of a beginner, and exercise herself in imitating our Lord's love of suffering. He suggested her making a general manifestation of her life, and with this suggestion she hastened to comply by writing to him; ending her letter with these words:

"My worthy master, sinner that I am, I prostrate myself at your feet. I beg of your loving heart to lead me to the heart of God, and I beg of you to take me for your child in time and in eternity."

From this moment there sprang up between these two a most beautiful spiritual friendship, such a one as that between Blessed Diana and Blessed Jordan of Saxony.

Though Suso was one of the gentlest and most lovable of men, his gentleness did not preclude firmness. He sent Elsbeth a copy of Cassian's *Conferences* and, urged by the account of the terrific austerities of the Fathers of the Desert, she tried to imitate them. But as soon as Henry learnt of this he utterly forbade her continuing in such a course. If Elsbeth thirsted after suffering, she would receive her fill, for God would send all that was necessary for her salvation; and she could be certain that what he sent would prove much more searching and efficacious than any she might choose for herself.

Some of his most beautiful letters are written to her.

I know, O Lord, that it accords with thy nature to love those who are like thee; for I know that the kingdom of heaven is none else than thy love. That is why thou continually formest me in thy likeness, whether through sorrow or joy, through pleasure or pain. O Lord, my gentle well-beloved Lord, it is thy hands that gather for me whatever sufferings come upon me; if the world despises me, then am I worthy of thy love. What an exchange is this! If thou sendest sufferings thou rewardest them by thy love. O sweet sufferings, which bring the love of my well-beloved Master. That is why I receive pain and sorrow with joy.

Elsbeth was delicate and she was often ill; but these recurrent illnesses became for her, as for so many, only a new opportunity of climbing higher up the mountain of God, the spiritual life. In fact she attained sanctity so rapidly that Suso himself was astonished. He gave her the reason:

It is because you have given yourself to God and are completely detached; because you have taken such unbounded trouble and have undergone so much bodily suffering in order to crush the old man, and to tread underfoot all false love. My child, a man who has never taken wine when he begins to drink feels the effect of it far more than does one who has often drunk his fill. By analogy, I think this is true in your case, by reason of the bright and sweet love of the Eternal Wisdom which has so taken possession of you. Perhaps God wishes to draw you and lead you ever higher to the inexhaustible source from which you have so far only tasted a drop. Perhaps he wishes to manifest his marvels in you, and the superabundance of his goodness. This is how you must act; you must throw yourself at his feet and renounce yourself; you must abandon yourself to his goodness without any return on yourself. Fear nothing, it is the loving attraction of God in the soul and it must needs be so. Still, you must watch your bodily forces, lest they be too much weakened. This you must do, and then you will fly upward easily, since all that might prevent your higher flight is taken away.

126

Her flight was a high one, for at last she attained the summit, the crown, mystic union; and after that Henry was able to offer her all the strength and beauty of the doctrine to be found in *The Little Book of Eternal Wisdom*. She died in 1360, five years before her spiritual father, and her end was as blest as her life had been. After her death she appeared in vision to Henry clad in shining garments, dazzling with light and heavenly joy. She came close to him and "showed him in what noble fashion she had passed into the pure Godhead." His soul was filled with heavenly consolation; but when he came to himself he sighed deeply, saying as he did so: "My God, how blessed is the man who strives after thee alone. He may well be content to suffer pains that thou rewardest in such a fashion. God help us to rejoice in this maiden, and in all his dear friends, and to enjoy his divine countenance eternally."

Elsbeth was not alone among her community in her pursuit of Eternal Wisdom, for she tells many another beautiful story of Suso's other friends among the Friends of God at the priory. Beli von Lutisbach had a very special devotion to the Mother of God, in whose honour she repeated fifty *aves* three times daily. Once when she was ill, as she lay in the infirmary, our Lady appeared to her clad in dazzling white, and seated herself on the sick sister's bed. When Beli asked her who she was she answered:

"I am the heavenly Mother whom you have so often honoured, and this white garment is the one you have woven for me with those angelic salutations which you have so often repeated."

Beli then noticed that the robe had no sleeves, and when she asked why the robe was sleeveless, our Lady replied:

"Every day you say fifty times the *ave* three times over, if you will say yet another fifty, you will finish the robe you have made."

Mezzi Sidwibrin was old when she entered at Töss. She was simple and a little odd, but her soul, as her works and words showed, was full of the most tender love of God. She received a special grace to give herself with great zeal to the everyday duties of her life. She used to shed tears of joy when she spun flax or wool at being thus permitted to serve the servants of God in his holy house. And as she worked she would speak of our Lord as if he were actually present with them. Sometimes she would say: "O Lord, I am confident that thou wilt give me a soul for every thread that I spin to thy honour." And as she spoke tears of joy would roll down her cheeks.

Such souls did not enter religious life just as a matter of convenience. When Elsbeth Bechlin was only eight years old, in a dream she saw herself in the place where her father, Saint Dominic, had seen his children gathered, namely, under the mantle of the Blessed Virgin, and she received a promise that she should never leave this secure refuge.

When she was ten years old she told her father that she wished to be a Dominican but this did not fit in with his plans for her and so he began to put all manner of obstacles in her way. Elsbeth was not to be deterred, and she told her father: "If you give me to the world I shall stand as witness against you in the Day of Judgement." At the age of eleven she entered at the Priory of Töss.

Adelheit von Frauenburg had been married to a great noble, but God gave her the grace to find nothing but bitterness in the riches and pleasures of the world. She desired none but God the only good and so she begged of him the grace to leave the world, even if, in order to make this possible, he struck her with leprosy. For many years she lived in great dignity and luxury, but even so she found time and opportunity to spend long hours in prayer. After the death of her husband her parents wished her to marry again and she had much to suffer in consequence before she gained the desire of her heart and became a nun at Töss.

The spiritual life of the nuns at Töss was centred in Christ crucified. They did not look on the Passion as something which was over and done with; for them Christ did not suffer on a certain day in a certain year in the far-off country of Judea. He was crucified daily, there in Töss in their very midst. Daily at the seven canonical hours of the divine office, from matins to compline, they were with our Lord; in the Garden of Olives, before the tribunal of Pilate, in the court where he was tortured by the soldiery. With the daughters of Jerusalem they accompanied him on the way of the Cross; they assisted at his death; with his blessed Mother they remained at the foot of the Cross on which he died, and even after his burial they did not leave him. They tried as far as they could to realise the infinity of the love which had nailed their Spouse to the Cross. As our Lord told their spiritual Father Henry Suso:

It would be easier to bring back past days, to revive all faded flowers, to gather up every drop of rain that falls than to measure my love for thee and all men. And that is why I am so covered with the marks of love that there could not be found on the whole of my body one tiny spot which did not bear its own mark of love.

For this reason the nuns of Töss loved to contemplate all their Lord's unspeakable sufferings, these marks of love, especially the marks of the nails in his hands and feet and the lance-wound in his side; for they used to call them the love-tokens of their Spouse.

Elsbeth Bechlin was enabled to bear great sufferings without any human consolation by calling to mind a prayer which had been taught her by a holy priest, perhaps Henry of Nördlinger himself:

Lord, remember that your hands and your heart have been opened for me, and so you cannot refuse me the help of your grace.

Mechthilt von Stans was by nature a lover of pleasure, and this she was obliged to conquer in many a hard battle before she merited the courage to speak in this way to Jesus her only hope:

O Lord, my God, see that for the love of thee I have abandoned the world and everything which can give me joy and consolation. I beg thee, then, in thy infinite mercy and divine goodness to be pleased to be thyself my consolation, because thou well knowest that I have no other in this world.

For a long time she begged for this grace with great fervour. Then one night she saw coming towards her a celestial army. One of those whom she saw carried a Cross which shone like crystal, and he told Mechthilt to follow them to the church. She joined the procession who as they went sang the *Vexilla Regis*. When they reached the church one of the band of the Blessed offered the Cross for the rest to venerate. As she watched, the nun saw our Lord come down from heaven and place himself on the Cross; the others moved forward but she remained humbly in the background. Then our Lord looked lovingly at her saying:

"My sister, do you believe that I am true God and true Man?"

"Yes, Lord, I do believe it," answered Mechthilt.

"Come, then," said our Lord. So she came up to the Cross and the rest stood aside to give her room. When she was quite close, our Lord said again:

"Sister Mezzi, do you desire any other consolation than myself alone?"

"No, Lord," replied the nun. Then said our Lord:

"Since you desire no other consolation than myself and have for my sake renounced all other joys, I myself will console you with my sacred body, my precious blood, my soul and my divinity. You shall receive the consolation that I gave my beloved disciples on Holy Thursday and I myself will take charge of you, both your body and your soul. There is no one so dear to me to whom I will entrust the care of you, I will care for you myself; and understand that my consolations will never be lacking. Although trouble will find an entry into your heart, you will find me there at the same time to be your consolation and your joy. My well-beloved, my chosen one, know that the kingdom of heaven will be yours when you leave this world. I give you my eternal benediction."

Then our Lord left Mechthilt all on fire with divine grace and the desire of heaven. But, true lover of her Spouse, she could not rest content with tasting the divine sweetness only, and from the day that heaven was promised to her she longed to experience the pain of the five wounds, so that she might show in some degree her love for our Lord and her gratitude for the favours he had granted her.

Yet while these mystics, following the footsteps of Suso, reached the heights of the contemplative life—the "great silent darkness," "the shining and transfigured obscurity" where words can convey no more than the faintest reflection —the roots of their spirituality were buried deeply in the fundamental reality of that law which rules all those who desire to fly from sin and live a Christian life.

When Margaret Finkin came to die, her sister asked her to tell them of the graces she had received from God, and she answered:

"It seems to me enough that God has given me the grace to do without weariness what it is my duty to do, and to keep the rule with joy."

Jutzi Schulthasin heard an interior voice which told her: "You must regulate your life according to faith, and know that this is the best and surest way."

Elsbeth Bechlin, who had held the Infant Jesus in her arms, asked for no particular graces in her prayer, for she said:

"The safest way we can follow is to keep ourselves from sin and practise virtue."

As Friar Henry wrote to a prior, his friend:

Perfection does not consist in consolation, but rather in the submission of our wills to God, above all in desolation. Let us remember that the obedience of our Lord was perfect when his mouth and tongue burned with the fever of his wounds, and this was only increased and his thirst became greater when they gave him gall and vinegar to drink. We must understand that we should have more esteem for a soul who is submissive in desolation and aridity than for one who is enjoying the sensible delights of devotion.

CHAPTER XVIII

THE FATHER

As we have already seen, in the time of Friar Henry there were two types of convents; there were communities of fervent women like those of Töss and Engelthal, and there were those which were merely a refuge for girls who for some reason or other were unable to marry. There was very little discipline in many of this latter type of convent and the young nuns there lived as easy a life as they could, often with results which were the reverse of edifying.

Henry interested himself not only in communities of the fervent, but, true to his vocation both as a Dominican and as a friend of God, he did all in his power to reform those which were relaxed. His influence being stronger with the individual than with a number, he endeavoured to raise the standard of ideal in the whole convent through the young nuns whose personality made them the natural leaders; sometimes he was successful, sometimes he was not.

In one of these convents there was a young nun whom he had tried for a long while to influence. She was not bad at heart, but very pretty, very vain, very frivolous—queening it over a band of youths and maidens as empty-headed as herself. Friar Henry was accustomed to speak to her in very plain terms. His words frightened and humbled her, and

132

she always promised to amend her ways; but the impression left by his exhortations quickly faded, and she invariably dropped back into her old manner of life.

At last, finding that he only wasted words, Henry said to her:

"Daughter, for the last time I warn you to leave off these practices. I tell you that if you will not do so willingly and cheerfully, you will be constrained to do so unwillingly and with sadness."

The girl looked quickly up at the friar, startled and scared:

"I will do as you tell me," she said, and then added with a smile, "but I do not believe your threats all the same."

But Henry could not let it rest at that. If he was unable to save the girl by his words, he would see what deeds would do. So going into the friars' church he knelt at the foot of the crucifix and there took a severe discipline, praying the while for the salvation of this soul, no matter what the cost.

His prayer was heard, but certainly not in the manner that the object of his solicitude would have wished. The young nun was taken ill and confined to her bed for months. When she began to get about again, it was to find that she had become deformed and hunch-backed. She had utterly lost the beauty and grace of which she was so vain, and was now so hideous and repulsive to look at that she was constrained to live the hidden life she had refused to live for the love of God.

In this same community was another young nun, high-born, high-spirited and beautiful. When she saw what had happened to her companion she feared Henry's influence so greatly that, not having the slightest desire to live a stricter kind of life, and desiring still less to be afflicted with any deformity, she refused to have anything to do with him or even to come near him.

Her elder sister, also a nun in the same convent, but devout and earnest, did her best to persuade her young sister, if she would do no more, at least to meet the friar in the presence of others. But the girl was emphatic in her refusal, declaring that nothing should induce her to have anything to do with him. At last, seeing that she gained nothing by her importunity, the elder sister went herself to the friar to beg him to contrive somehow to meet her younger sister in such a way that she could not escape him. Henry promised to do his best.

One morning all the younger members of the community went out into one of the fields to pick flax. The friar saw them leave the house and followed the party. He came on his quarry suddenly as she was stooping over her work, and made some commonplace remark. In an instant she was aflame with passion.

"It is a waste of your time and mine to talk to me," she flared out, "I am not changing my way of life for you or anyone else. It is no use for you to talk to me of confession, for you cannot make me go. I had rather be buried alive than exchange my good time for the dead-and-alive existence that you and your devotees lead."

She flounced off, and her companions horrified at her rudeness and vehemence followed remonstrating. Whatever she felt, there was no need to behave so discourteously to the famous friar. She was not bound to follow his advice but she had no right to give the community a bad name by behaving so rudely in public. Their reproaches merely added fuel to the flame, and she became so abusive that Henry could do nothing but go away as quickly as possible.

He went into the convent chapel and there began to pray for this fiery-tempered young sinner, asking God to show him what he could do. As he walked out he came face to face with one of the nuns who had been present that morning. With flaming cheeks she began to stammer excuses but Henry stopped her for he knew that this was the chance he had been praying for.

"Can you help me?" he asked. "I want to meet your companion in a place where she cannot escape me."

"I think I can manage it," she answered. "We are going to the courtyard this evening with the flax we picked this morning to separate it for spinning. If you will wait in the parlour yonder we shall pass the door, and it will go hard if I do not find a way of pushing her in to you."

Accordingly, she walked that evening to the courtyard beside the young nun, and as they passed the parlour door she opened it quickly, and before she knew what was happening, pushed her in, shut the door on her, and ran away. Seeing she was fairly trapped, and a little ashamed of her rudeness in the morning, but still determined to hold out, the young nun crossed to the window-seat and sat down with her back to the room, staring out of the window. Henry stood in silence for a moment and then he began to speak to the unresponsive back.

"Beautiful and gentle maiden," he said, "God's chosen one! How long will you abandon your lovely body and your tender heart to the vile and wicked devil? You are so richly adorned by the everlasting God with every grace that it is indeed an evil fate that such a noble maiden should be the beloved of any other save the all-adorable One alone. Who has a greater right to pluck the fair and tender rose than he to whom it belongs? No, dear, lovely maiden, open your bright falcon eyes and think of that beautiful chosen love which begins here and lasts for ever and ever. Think, too, what sorrow and unfaithfulness, what pain and suffering both in body and in possessions, in soul and honour, they must needs endure, willingly or unwillingly, who pursue earthly love; only they are so blinded by the honeyed poison that they forget the great hurt which follows from this in time and in eternity. Come, then, maiden, whose form is as beautiful as an angel, whose heart is high and noble, turn thy nature's high nobility to him who is noble from eternity, and cease from this disastrous way of life. I promise thee on

135

my honour, that God will take thee for his darling, will be altogether true to thee, and will love thee right well, here and hereafter, in time and in eternity."

As the friar spoke the grace of God touched the soul of the girl. She turned to face him, and for a moment sat silent while tears ran down her cheeks. Then, mastering her emotion, she stood up and speaking in a low tone but with determination, she answered:

"Father, I give myself this day to God and to you; and from now on I renounce the free wild life I have led. With your help and counsel, I will give myself to the God of love, to be his own, and his only until death." She paused again. Then suddenly a flood of joy poured over her soul in the realisation that she had at last done what her conscience knew to be right, and with radiant face raised upward she cried aloud: "This is the hour of my joy; and may the kind Lord, who is waiting to receive back the wanderers who return to him, be praised for evermore."

Meanwhile her companions were standing outside the door, waiting anxiously for her return, greatly afraid lest the friar should rob them of the one who led them in every frolic. When the minutes began to pass into hours and still she did not appear they grew more and more restless, until at last, unable to bear it any longer, they called to her to come out to them. At this she rose at once and went to the door. On the threshold she paused, making no movement to join them. "Come," they urged her. "You've been serious for long enough."

The young nun smiled and shook her head.

"Come," they urged again. "Come and forget your serious thoughts," and they seized her by the hand to draw her out. Disengaging herself she answered gently:

"Good-bye, my friends, good-bye and God bless you! For from now on I will have no friend but the faithful God. Everything else must go in exchange for the love he offers me."

From this time on, in fulfilment of her promise, her whole life was changed, and as she had formerly been the leader in every frivolous amusement so now she was foremost in the fervent service of God; a model of every religious virtue until her death.

Friar Henry remained her faithful friend, visiting her from time to time, encouraging her to perseverance and comforting her if she were sick or in sorrow. Once when he was battling with many difficulties to come to her help in time of need God helped him by a miracle.

The journey was a long and difficult one, and Henry was really ill. Through marshy plains and over steep hills he struggled, and as he journeyed along what must have been a veritable *via crucis,* he lifted his heart to God, saying within himself:

"Merciful God, be mindful of the painful steps thou didst take for man's salvation, and keep my child safe." At times he found the going so hard that he was obliged to support himself on his young companion's arm. Once, when it seemed as if he could go no farther, his companion said to him:

"Father, God should have considered how ill you are, and should have sent you a horse to ride until you came near some town or village where passing drivers would certainly have given you a lift."

"Well, if we both ask God for it," replied Henry, smiling, "I am certain that he will reward your virtue by granting your desire."

As he spoke there appeared, trotting out from the wood on the right-hand side of the path, a fine horse, saddled and bridled but without a rider. At the sight of the animal the other friar cried out:

"See, father, God has not forsaken you but has come to your help."

"Son," answered Henry, "look about you on all sides and see whether there is anyone to whom the horse can belong."

The other scanned the plain before him looking on all sides but there was no living being in sight save only the horse trotting towards them. So the brother returned to Henry saying earnestly:

"Truly, father, God has sent it to you, for there is no other living being in sight. I beg of you, mount and ride."

Henry rose from his seat. He did not, however, approach the horse but stood waiting by the wayside.

"Brother," he said, "if the horse stops when it reaches us, I trust in God that he has sent it here for our necessity." As he spoke the horse trotted up and stood quietly before him, so he said:

"So be it in God's name." Then his companion helped him to mount and walked beside him, leading the horse, until the pair reached the outskirts of a village, and Henry was well rested. The friar then dismounted and, laying the reins on the animal's neck, allowed it to return whence it had come. But whose it was, or how it had appeared in answer to his need, he never discovered.

Some of his letters to his spiritual children in convents are still extant. This is one that he wrote to a nun who, helped by God's grace and his direction, had turned from tepidity to fervour.

Your return to God, my dear sister, has given me such joy that I cannot contain myself; with all the love of my soul I bless Mary the glorious Queen of Heaven, who has enlightened your heart and soul with her gentle radiance. I am carried out of myself with joy. I seem to myself to have found my way to the golden age, and to be walking in the garden of paradise. I am calling on the birds of heaven, and the swans who float on the ocean of light, to praise God for the grace he has bestowed on you, and through you on me. Come, then, holy angels, who live in the home of glory, come and rejoice with me. What rapture, what rejoicing, what songs of praise re-echo through heaven, for a soul has returned to God.

Yes! A child of God was lost and is found, was dead and has returned to life. Behold a rose garden which wild beasts had ravaged and destroyed, is now covered in divine beauty, and is blossoming with countless heavenly lilies and roses. The savage beasts have been put to flight; and the garden is now enclosed and guarded. This garden was stolen from its Master and trampled under foot, now it has been given back to him and is yielding a rich harvest of flowers. And so, ye musicians of Paradise, take your harps and your psalteries, all your musical instruments, and, in Jerusalem the Blessed, sing a new canticle to the glory of God. Behold, this spouse of Christ has cast from her heart every impure passion, she has thrown from her the joyous crown which wreathed her hair, she has banished all earthly love, she has cast from her the poisoned cup which she was wont to drain so greedily.

O deceitful world, O impure and sinful love, depart to hide thy head under the ashes of shame. Thou hast been conquered, and it is God and we weak creatures who are the victors. Do you not see that this barren tree of the wilderness has become a fertile and godly one? Let the heavens rejoice, and the blessed in heaven make merry, singing: "Glory be to God!" This is not the least beautiful of thy works, O Lord; neither is it the least worthy of thy goodness, since the storm of thy terrible justice has given way to calm. Let us sing to God a mighty act of thanksgiving.

A ferocious, dangerous she-wolf has become a meek and gentle lamb. Thy child's soul was wounded, tortured by remorse, loaded under the heavy chains of sin. Her conscience was filled with anguish, bitterness, all manner of sufferings. See her now, filled with an infinitely greater joy than any the world has to offer; free and without care she flies heavenward; and now she can no longer understand how she was able to live for one moment in the dark and obscure night of earthly love. This, O my God, is the proof of all thou hast taught me. Whilst an upright soul and carefree heart is set towards eternity, swiftly the pure flames of thy divine love come to embrace it. Here, O good Jesus, is a transformation, the work of thy omnipotent hand. Here, O Mary, is the work of thy immense compassion.

My very dear daughter, when we forsake the errors of the world, to go to God, we must so regulate our lives that nothing can turn us from the chosen path. If a poor peasant, if an innkeeper's servant were loved and espoused by a prince, would she not feel the most faithful love and the greatest zeal in his service? And would not the remembrance of her own unworthiness be a perpetual spur to her ardour? For this reason we sinners should strive to surpass the saints and those who have not sinned. O, how much we could do if we were as eager in the service of God as we were wont to be in the service of the world. If we have endured so much in the pursuit of sin is it not simple justice that we should suffer in order to gain heaven?

O Eternal Wisdom, if men could but look on thee with the eyes of their soul as I behold thee, would not all earthly love vanish at once? What would I not do that all might give themselves to thee alone, and so rest in the abyss of thy bounty? The slaves of this world hide their deformity under the mask of deceit, cover with a hypocritical splendour all that is vicious and ugly in them. Tear away their mask.

Thou, on the contrary, O divine Wisdom, only showest thy servants that which appears difficult and wearisome, hiding from them all thy delights. Why dost thou act so if it were not, O good God, to allow us some merit for our action, in order to lead us through passing troubles to the crown of joy and eternal peace? My sweet Jesus, lovest thou me? Dost thou cherish me and hast thou received me among the number of thy friends? The thought of my happiness fills me with joy. If I dared desire and ask for something, could I desire or ask for anything more precious, more sublime, than the moment when Jesus will show me the beauty of his countenance and give me the kiss of infinite peace? Who can doubt that he will be our paradise? Thy eyes, my Jesus, are more sparkling than the rays of the sun, thy mouth is gracious and distils honey; thy countenance is like the lily and the rose, and thy virginal beauty in its entirety infinitely surpasses all that the world holds beautiful, joyous and desirable. The more I stretch beyond time and earthly things in contemplating thee, the more in my ecstasy and joy I find thee to be admirable. The more I experience thee the more I realise how good thou art, how gentle, how lovable. "Such is my beloved and he is my friend." How happy you are my dear daughter if you have Christ for your friend. Farewell.

Here is an extract from a letter to a novice who is tempted to return to the world:

Be strong and indomitable in God, my daughter; and never allow yourself to be led astray by the arts of the devil. I know well that just now your soul is enduring sharp agony, terrible temptations; but if you have courage you will win through this difficult moment, and will soon reach the fields, the tranquil meadows of a peaceful spiritual life. I wish I could fight in your stead receiving in my own soul the attacks and the wounds that you are enduring. But if I could do that then you would not receive in heaven, with Christ's other soldiers, the palm of victory; for all the temptations which are bearing you down are only the occasions of victory, and they will become the precious jewels which will adorn your heavenly crown. Resist the devil courageously; the combat will be short, and your glory will be eternal if you only surmount the trials and difficulties of your novitiate.

CHAPTER XIX

THE FRIEND

MONKS and friars as well as nuns called Henry Suso father, and to all he broke the bread of mystical doctrine. Very few names of his personal friends are known, in part probably because the friar was by temperament a solitary soul, a wayfarer through life, in part because our chief source of information is his own interior life written by himself. He does speak, however, of sinners with whom he came in contact, and that is apt to leave an impression that his only dealings with his fellow men were when he either converted them or suffered persecution at their hands. His connection with the Friends of God must have led to many a close and enduring friendship; but of these, except in the case of Elsbeth Stagel, we have no record.

Among these friends of his was a monk holding a high position in his own Order. God had laid on this man heavy interior suffering, which oppressed him so greatly that at last he came to the priory at Ulm to ask help from his friend. Henry promised to pray for him and suggested his making a short stay at the priory.

It happened one daydawn, not long after, that the friar was seated in his little chapel opening out of the choir, praying for his friend, when suddenly he saw the devil as a hideous swarthy figure with fiery eyes, standing in the doorway of the choir holding a bow and a quiver of flaming arrows. Henry spoke to him.

"I adjure thee by the living God to tell me who thou art and what thou art doing here?"

"I am the spirit of blasphemy," answered the fiend.

As soon as the evil one had spoken these words, Henry glanced across the choir to see his friend the monk coming in at the cloister door on his way to mass. Then the fiend, fixing one of the fiery arrows to his bow, shot the monk right through the heart. As the arrow struck him he fell back and could not enter the choir. On seeing this, Henry became very angry and cried out, rebuking the fiend; whose only answer was to draw out another arrow and take aim at the friar himself. But quick as thought, Henry turned in spirit to his heavenly mother, crying out to her:

"O Virgin Mary, bless me with thy gentle babe." And immediately the power of the devil departed and he vanished straight away.

When the hour of prime and mass was over, Henry went in search of his friend to comfort him, telling him at the same time what remedies would be of service to his soul. This is what he told him, contained in his sermon, *Lectus noster floridus*, which is still extant.

Those who wish to live a spiritual life must not fancy that they can make progress in virtue unless they first apply themselves to gaining peace of mind and conscience. Jesus Christ loves to rest in pure tranquil consciences, a fact which it is easy to understand. . . . The delights of the Word made flesh are in those whose hearts are made pure by peace of conscience. This the spouse in the Canticle understood when she said, *Lectus noster floridus*, that is to say, our dwelling is peaceful and the bed of our love decked with flowers. Come then, O Lord, my beloved, for my soul is closed to all other love; my conscience is clean and adorned with the lilies of virtue; my heart is calm and at peace. I desire thy presence only, desire that thou mayest take me to the bosom of thy infinite love, and that there I may sleep and take my rest.

Understand, then, how scrupulous souls, for ever tormented by doubts and inquietude, have hearts which are ill prepared to receive Jesus Christ. In place of that peace which religion is meant to give, these souls make their lives miserable, full of trouble and temptation. . . .

These are three of the chief sources of danger: the first is a disordered sadness; the second is an exaggerated disturbance of soul; the third is profound discouragement. In respect to the first, you must know that at times a man finds himself so overwhelmed by melancholy that not only does he lose all taste for good, but he cannot even carry out his good intentions; he lives in ignorance of what is wanting to him, and cannot understand the source of his trouble. . . . But abide in hope and do not give way to discouragement, for soon the time will return when you will again serve God with joy.

It is true that melancholy often has its source in temperament, but that does not make it less deplorable for people, after beginning to serve God with ardour, later to relinquish the struggle overcome by sadness and inertia. It is however hardly surprising, since constancy and fortitude are never more necessary than at the beginning of the struggle against vice. [The saint then explains how such sadness is the fault of the soul itself; then he says:] I will explain by an example.

There was once a servant of God, a friend of the Eternal Wisdom, who in the beginning of his conversion was subject to such deep fits of melancholy that not only did he lose all taste for prayer and reading, but was so paralysed in will that he seemed unable to act. One day, when he was in his room almost beside himself, he heard an interior voice say: "Why do you remain sorrowful and idle? Why do you stay here eating out your heart? Why do you lie crushed under these miseries? Have courage! Get up, do violence to yourself; meditate on my Passion and cruel sufferings. So you will dissipate your sadness." The servant of God obeyed. Meditation on the Passion of Christ drove out sadness, and by continuing in the holy exercise, he cured himself of his disposition to melancholy.

The second temptation is an exaggerated disturbance of spirit. Those who experience this temptation know why they fail; they realise that their wills are not sufficiently conformed to that of God, since they experience a crowd of natural desires, often opposed to God's good pleasure. The root of the evil lies in too great an esteem of unworthy objects . . ., and they feel this most deeply when, desiring to be recollected, they are assailed by wicked and shameful thoughts against him and his goodness. This is the most painful temptation which can assail a man, not on account of the evil, for the soul does not consent, but because of the grief it causes the sufferer.

To this temptation are often joined those against faith, hateful thoughts against God and his saints; the tempted soul is assailed by mad thoughts of suicide and of despair of the divine mercy. . . . Despair comes from one of three sources; either the soul does not know what God is, or it does not understand what sin is, or it does not realise what contrition of heart is. God is an inexhaustible source of infinite mercy and sovereign tenderness. No mother could snatch her child from a burning building more swiftly than God is constrained to succour a penitent soul, even though it should have committed every sin in the world a thousand times over. . . .

Let the soul which is in sorrow or temptation gather its powers within it and meditate on what God is, then it can never question his mercy. Let it also try to understand the nature of sin—that unless the will is set and deliberate there is no sin; neither is there if reason opposes temptation, and if the evil thoughts which present themselves are repugnant to it. There is sin only when, with the full knowledge and by the fully consenting act of the will, without hesitation or repugnance, the soul yields itself to the evil suggestion.

. . . Let the afflicted soul apply itself to understanding the virtue and power of contrition. True, humble, trusting contrition delivers a man from all his sins. A contrite and humble heart always obtains mercy. It is written: " My son, in thy infirmity do not despise thyself, but pray to the Lord and he will care for thee."

Scrupulous people distress themselves in many ways; for, in a manner of speaking, they believe no one, and no counsel brings calm to their troubled souls. Moreover, they keep returning to their sins and doubts, and the more they think of them the more they aggravate the trouble. They should rest content with one good confessor, and trust themselves entirely to his judgement and direction. At the Day of Judgement, while the confessor must give an account of his direction of the penitent, the penitent himself is shielded behind his obedience and submission to his confessor. . . .

Those who give way to disordered fear and scrupulosity

become angry with God just as those do who are wanting in resignation in adversity. They are like horses who have not yet become used to the control of the bridle and who strain and hurt themselves in their efforts to fight against it. The more such people struggle against their troubles the more painful will they find them. Their only remedy is to abandon themselves to the will of God, whose eyes of mercy are always fixed on our trials, and on our patience under them, in order to preserve us from evil. . . .

[Prayer is at times a difficulty.] Painful and difficult prayer is more pleasing to God than one which is easy and tranquil. The grief and pain of one who tries in vain to pray, lamenting his inability to do so, makes him a victor in God's sight and obtains for him abundant graces.

You will ask me, perhaps, how God permits persons consecrated to him to be subjected to such interior trials and, above all, to such terrible temptations to despair that bodily pains are as nothing in comparison. There are those who, in their ignorance of the secrets of divine Wisdom, pretend that despair can have no other cause than sin; but this error is easily refuted by the experience of persons of great innocence and holiness of life who suffer such temptations for years at a time, for these temptations do not torment worldly folk and sinners, but rather those who fear the divine majesty.

Souls enlightened by grace who submit to this trial in expiation of their sins ought to bless and thank God who does not allow sinners to live as they will, but who punishes and purifies them in accordance with his goodness and mercy. It is, however, God's own secret why his divine wisdom employs such chastisements for the humiliation and punishment of sinners. He knows the heart of each one, his habits and inclinations, and foresees his needs in a thousand different ways according to his good pleasure.

It is certain that the fruit of such temptations is very abundant. In the first place, men who are by nature proud can in no way better acquire humility, the true mother of all virtues; because when a man sees himself full of evil and debasing thoughts he is driven to know himself and to lower himself beneath all others. Nothing is more useful to him, for it is impossible that God should allow the loss and ruin of a humble soul. Moreover, he who lives interiorly nailed to the cross should cherish it, and rest at our Lord's feet, thanking his infinite goodness which, by means of these temptations to despair, draws him back from hell, delivers him from a multitude of sins, sets him free from all love of the vanities of the world, and lays up for him treasures of merit in heaven. The more painful the trials sent by God, the more those who suffer them learn to love and study virtue. No way of escaping the danger they fear seems impossible since they hope to deliver themselves from the temptation which weighs them down, and which God permits in order that they may exercise themselves in good works and reach their goal at last full of grace and merits.

We must, then, admire the designs of divine wisdom which disposes all things with strength and sweetness in our souls. That which seems our misfortune, leading to damnation, may be changed under the strong guidance of our Father into a means of holiness and merit, leading to our salvation and abundant glory in heaven.

Let me add finally that this temptation to interior shame, blasphemy and despair places those who resist it in a certain fashion, in the ranks and with the prerogatives of martyrs; for God's servants would greatly prefer to give their lives for Jesus Christ at a single stroke, rather than to suffer such painful interior temptations for months, even years. So we may conclude that persons who suffer from scruples are the most favoured by divine love, and the most certain of reaching heaven when they bear this trial in patience and humility. Scrupulous souls die continually, they suffer a perpetual purgatory, and so they leave the earth to fly to heaven purified and free from sins to expiate. This is what happened to a holy soul who had been cruelly tried by this temptation; God glorified it at the moment of death and led it to heaven without passing through the flames of purgatory. To the praise and honour of Jesus Christ, who is blessed for ever, I am able to give witness of the eternal salvation of this soul.

Among the many people who sought Friar Henry's help there came one from a foreign country who had so far lost courage in a long fight against temptation that he at last made up his mind to commit suicide.

In his desperation he left home one dark night with the intention of throwing himself into the river which ran swift and deep quite close at hand. As he stood on the bank, bracing himself for the plunge, he distinctly heard a voice speaking to him.

"Stop!" cried the voice. "Damn not your soul, but go seek my servant Henry, of the Friars Preachers, who will draw you out of the gulf of despair."

Filled with a new hope the man went home, fetched a wallet and staff, and set out at once in search of this man, a stranger even in name. For days and weeks he journeyed until one evening he came by chance to Ulm, to learn that the friar he was seeking lived there. Next morning he set out again on his return journey, strengthened in soul and instructed how to avoid such temptations for the future.

The loving servant of the divine Wisdom could never bear to shut his heart against any who were in trouble. One day, when he happened to be in difficulties himself, he chanced to pass a house from which there issued the most pitiful sounds of grief, shrill cries, loud wailing and lamentations. Instantly, forgetting his own troubles, Henry hurried into the house to see if he could be of service. In the living-room he found a woman dishevelled and seemingly half-distraught, her face all swollen with crying, as she sat rocking herself and wailing. Henry, full of pity, hurried up to her asking:

"Dear lady, what has happened to you? What is your trouble that you are bewailing yourself so grievously."

Between her sobs the woman made answer:

"I have let a needle fall and cannot find it anywhere."

Henry stared at her for one moment speechless, and then turning on his heel left the house. There was really nothing else for him to do.

CHAPTER XX

THE SAINT

ALTHOUGH Friar Henry's life at Ulm was busy, peaceful, and successful even according to human standards, the wheels did not always run smoothly. He did not wish it, for he was too deeply in love with the Cross to desire anything different from his Saviour's chalice.

Once when life had been going very smoothly, far too smoothly for the liking of this great lover since for a whole month he had met with no difficulty of any kind, he happened to be visiting one of the convents where the nuns called him father. As was natural, the nuns began to ask him how things fared with him.

"I fear that matters are going very ill with me at present," he answered with a smile, "and for this reason. It is now four weeks since anyone has attacked me, either personally or through my good name, and, as you know, this is quite contrary to what usually happens to me. So I am beginning to fear that God has forgotten me."

He had hardly finished speaking when the portress came in to tell him that someone was waiting at the great door to tell him something. It proved to be one of his own lay-brethren who wished to have a personal word with him. As soon as Henry appeared the brother began:

"Father, I have only just left such a castle [naming it] where the prior had sent me on business. The Baron was at home and sent for me to ask very furiously where you might be found. When I asked him why he wanted you, he swore that your life was forfeit to him. And that is not the end of the business—for several of his kinsfolk, all soldiers, are searching all the monasteries round, hoping to find and kill you."

Henry smiled in genuine amusement.

"I should be glad to know," he said, "what I have done which deserves the death penalty."

"I can tell you that, if you want to know," replied the brother; "Mein Herr declares that you have persuaded his daughter to adopt a manner of life which she calls spiritual, and those who live that life are called spiritual persons. And he says that it is not only his daughter whom you have led

148

astray, but many more daughters of the nobility, and worst of all, this so-called spiritual life is in reality a most abandoned one. And there is more still, for while I was there a knight of the fiercest description came in, who swore with many oaths that you have robbed him of a beloved wife; for now she will no longer look at him but keeps her veil down, and her mind all turned on inward things. Whether or no this last is true, you are a better judge than I."

" Now praised be God," cried Henry, and having thanked the brother, sent him on his way. Then returning quickly to the parlour, he said gaily to the assembled nuns :

" Be of good cheer, my children, God has been mindful of me and has not forgotten me. Behold, there are many even now who are seeking my life." And he recounted to them the tale the brother had brought.

Though the Friar was growing old, he was still the Minnesinger; the lyre which had been attuned in the depths of his soul to the divine essence still sang the praises of the creation which its Creator had found good.

Once it happened that, after Henry had been for a long time contemplating the endless warfare between good and evil, and had begun to realise some of the marvels of divine goodness which were therein hidden, he spoke thus to God in his prayer :

My Lord, these sufferings are to outward appearance like a sharp thorn which pierces through flesh and bone. Therefore, my gentle Lord, grant that some fruit of good instruction may spring forth from these sharp thorns of suffering, in order that we, poor men, may suffer more patiently, and be the better enabled to offer up our sufferings to Thy praise and glory.

Then, his soul being rapt in ecstasy, God made answer :

I will show thee this day the high nobility of thy life, and how thou shouldst offer up thy sufferings to the praise and glory of God.

Then, in his boundless, heartfelt yearning, Friar Henry sang in thanksgiving a new canticle of praise; for his bodily senses were stilled in ecstasy, and the arms of his soul, as it were, stretched themselves forth out of the unfathomable fullness of his heart to the far-off ends of the universe, even from earth to heaven.

Lord, I hitherto have praised thee in contemplation
With the aid of the pleasantness of creatures,
  Their joyousness and song.
Now my soul finds expression in a far different chant;
Chant of a beauty heretofore unknown,
  The joyous song of suffering.

From my heart's depths I pray
  That my own sorrow and pain,
And the woe and anguish of every other human heart,
  Their smarting wounds
  And pangs of sickness,
The tears and groans of sad hearts,
  The misery of crushed hearts,
  The wailing of widows,
  Sighs of orphans,
  The hunger and want of the poor,
  The outpoured blood of martyrs,
And the holocaust of young hearts, with their gay desire to
  plan their life as they will,
  With the penances of thy friends,
  Pains and sorrows known and hid,
Which from now to the world's end I and all mankind
  must bear,
May spring up a source of unending praise
  To the unbegotten Father,
To the everlasting honour of thy Son who died on rood.
  And to this day do I, thy servant
  Desire to stand before thy face
In the stead of all sufferers who, perchance, have failed to
  turn
Their pains to bliss, by gratitude and patience,
Praising God for all ills his love may lay on them;
  And I desire to make offering of their pains,
  Whether they bear them well or ill;

Making in the desires of my heart, their sufferings my
   sufferings.
Each instant do I offer them to the sole-begotten Son
      In everlasting praise to his name,
      And for their own comfort;
Whether they are still robed in mortality
      Or beyond the grave in the hand of God.

Look on me, all ye who suffer, and listen.
We as Christ's members should be consoled,
Rejoicing that God, the sole-begotten Son
Our saviour and our head, suffered for us.
O Christ, be gracious to thy members,
And when through weakness patience fails
      Do thou fill up the lack.
Thou hast said to one who served thee:
      "Take courage and look on me;
I was once both noble and poor; tender and in misery;
Born out of the fullness of joys, yet full of grief."
Therefore, as valiant knights of our Lord
      Lose we not heart;
As noble followers of Christ our leader,
      Let us rejoice in pain.
If suffering brings no gain but this
      That by our griefs and pains
We grow in closer likeness to our mirror, Christ,
      Still every cross is gain.
      In very truth I think
That even if God should choose to give the same reward
      To those who suffer
And to those who bear but few afflictions,
Yet we should still choose affliction for our lot
      In likeness of our head;
For love begets likeness
And a burning love of the beloved.

But how do we dare, O Lord,
To mirror thyself in us in our small pains?
For the difference between thy sufferings and ours is
   infinite,
      Since thou alone, not we, have not deserved to suffer.
Who are we to cheat ourselves that in us the innocent
   suffer?

If we are guiltless in this one respect
        We merit punishment on other counts.
Therefore, we ring ourselves around thee, gentle Lover,
        Placing thee in our midst;
Spreading our thirsty veins far and wide,
Stretching with longing to thee, Fountain of all Grace.

        Christ, our head, look graciously on us,
Do thou fill the stinted measure of our frailty
        When patience fails us in affliction.
Even as the earth when most parched drinks deepest of rain
So, the more our guilt overwhelms us, the closer our out-
        stretched hearts clasp thee.
        We trust thy faithful promise
That the generous outpouring of thy blood will wash our
        souls
        Though our sins are as scarlet.
        In thanksgiving for thy bounty
We offer thee everlasting honour and praise;
And thy grace shall be our reward.
Since by thy almighty power,
All unlikeness to our Brother shall be taken away from us.

After the friar had remained for a long time motionless, drinking in this gracious sweetness, he came to himself and rose, thanking God and blessing him for the grace he had received.

One Easter Sunday, when Henry, in blithesome mood, sat for a short while rapt in contemplation according to his custom, he desired in his soul to learn what reward of joy those shall receive who in this life have borne many sufferings for Christ's sake. Then being seized with ecstasy, God flooded his soul with the light of understanding.

Let all who suffer with me rejoice,
        For their patience shall be gloriously rewarded;
And as here below they have been an object of pity to many
        So many shall rejoice eternally in the deserved praise and
        everlasting glory which shall be theirs.
They have died with me,
        And they shall also rise with me again in gladness.

Three special gifts will I give them; so precious that none
can reckon their value.

First,
I will give absolute power to their wishes in heaven and
on earth.

Second,
I will give them my divine peace, which neither angel
nor devil nor man, nor any other creature can ever
take away from them.

Third,
I will so inwardly kiss them through and through, and so
lovingly embrace them, that I in them and they in me,
and we together shall abide eternally, one undivided
unity for ever.

And since long waiting and praying are painful to restless
hearts,
This love shall not be withheld from them during this
short present hour of life, which lasts but for a
moment.

But it shall begin even now and be enjoyed eternally so far
as man's mortal nature can in each case support it.

This revelation filled the friar's soul with joy, and he
cried within himself:

Let him who suffers come forward and complain. God knows
that, as for myself, it seems as if I have never known what it is
to suffer; though I know well enough what joy is. Power both
to wish and to obtain my wish are given to me; a thing which
many an erring heart must be without. What more can I want?
Eternal Truth! show me this hidden mystery, in so far as I am
able to understand it, for it is a truth of which many men are
altogether ignorant.

Then was knowledge of this mystery given to the friar,
and in the explanation he received are made clear many
things in his own life which it is difficult to understand.

Man must begin with death to self and detachment from all
creatures, and there are few who have learnt this lesson. When
self is quite dead, the thoughts of such a one pass so completely
into God that he knows nothing of himself, except, as it were,
as he sees himself and all things in God, the fountainhead;

therefore, he has the same joy in all the acts of God as if it were granted to him to carry out everything according to his own will, while God stood by unconcerned with it.

Thus, such a man's will is absolute in power, for heaven and earth serve him, and every creature is subject to him in what it does and leaves undone. He feels no sorrow of heart about anything, for pain and sorrow of heart are only caused by constraint of the will. Externally, he has a sense of pain and pleasure as others have, and such is in him perhaps even more intense, because of his great tenderness; but in his inmost soul it finds no abiding place, and exteriorly he remains firm against impatience. He is filled with joy, even here below; for, being detached from self, his joy is complete and stable in all things. For in the divine essence into which his heart has passed away and become merged—that is, supposing he has not gone astray from the right path—there is neither pain nor sorrow but only peace and joy. If his human frailty leads him to commit sin, from whence spring pain and sorrow, then only will he find a flaw in his happiness. But if he avoids sin, and goes out from self-love, passing into that region where he will suffer neither pain nor sorrow—since there pain is not pain nor sorrow sorrow—then of a truth all will be well with him because all this follows the abnegation of self-will.

Such a man is driven with a great thirst towards God's will and his justice. He finds God's will so sweet and delightful, and he takes such pleasure in all God's ordinances, that he has no desire for anything else. This does not mean that he is forbidden to ask things from God, or to pray to him; but it has reference to the due and rightful going forth of his own judgement and will into the will of the supreme Godhead.

But a question arises: How does a man know God's will? God is superessential good, he is more interiorly present to a thing than that thing can be to itself; and against his will nothing can happen, neither can anything exist for an instant. Therefore the man who is for ever struggling against God's will, desiring his own if he could have it, must be utterly miserable. He has the kind of peace which is in hell, for he is always heavy and sad of heart. A soul which is stripped of self has God's peace present to it at all times, both in prosperity and adversity; for he who is all and does all is truly within it. Therefore, the sight of its own suffering cannot be grievous to such a soul, since thus he finds God, sees God, makes use of God's will and knows nothing of his own will; and this is not to speak of the consoling illuminations and heavenly delights with which God often sustains his suffering friends.

These persons are, as it were, in heaven; what happens or does not happen to them, what God does or does not do in all creatures, all turns to their advantage. And thus, he who can bear suffering well receives in this world a portion of the reward of his suffering; for he finds peace and joy in all things, and after death an everlasting life awaits him.

Once when in an ecstasy Henry found his guardian angel standing beside him, and turning to the bright spirit he spoke:

"Beloved spirit, whom God has given me for my guardian and consolation, I beg of you, by the love that you have for your Creator and your God, never leave me as long as I remain in this vale of tears."

"Why do you ask such a favour?" replied the angel. "Do you fear to trust yourself to God? Know and understand that from the bosom of eternity he has loved you, and he loves you now with so great a love that he wills never to leave you, and so it pleases him to dwell day and night in your heart."

Then the friar asked the angel to allow him to see how God dwelt in his heart; and the angel answered:

"Fix your eyes on your heart and you will see how the divine love operates within you."

Then the saint looking down saw that his breast was transparent as crystal; and he saw there, in the secret depths of his heart, the divine Wisdom resting in profound peace. By the side of his Beloved and leaning, like the beloved disciple, on his breast, was Henry's own soul, striving by this nearness to transform itself into a perfect likeness of the Eternal Wisdom, hiding itself in the arms of its divine redeemer, to rest there in the joy of ecstasy.

Once when the friar was on a journey, travelling this time in company with about twenty disciples, God worked a miracle to supply their wants. They had walked all day and when evening came they found themselves at a small hermitage on the outskirts of a hamlet. They set out the provisions they had brought with them, and were just going to sit down to table when they found that none of them had remembered to bring wine, and the water thereabouts was not fit to drink.

One or two of their number went into the village; but there was no wineshop and the folk had none to sell. They returned to the hut to find their company considerably augmented, for a number of people, hearing that the famous preacher was in the neighbourhood, had hurried there to see and hear him. They did not know what to do, for let alone the duty of hospitality to their new guests, they were all parched with thirst from their hot, dusty walk. As they were debating the matter, one of the women from the village appeared at the door with a bottle in her hand.

"I have just this one bottle left," said she, "but such as it is, you are welcome to it." Then glancing round at the number of people in the hut, she exclaimed in dismay: "But whatever good will this small bottle be among such a crowd of you?"

The friar, however, took the bottle from her and placed it on the table, thanking her with his usual gentle graciousness as he did so.

Then they all sat down, and his companions prayed him to bless the wine, and this he did very willingly in the mighty power of the lovely name of our Lord Jesus Christ. Then, being very thirsty, he lifted the bottle and drank; and after he had satisfied himself, he handed it to the man next him, and so on until all had quenched their thirst. After this the bottle was placed on the table in the sight of all and neither wine nor water was poured into it; for they had no more of the former, and the latter was unfit for drinking. The friar then began to speak to them and as they listened from time to time one or the other would pick up the bottle, and in this way they all drank again and again. But so absorbed were they in listening that no one noticed what

156

was happening. At last the friar finished speaking and the company came to earth once more. Then it occurred to them that they had drunk again and again from this one small bottle without emptying it, and they began to murmur one to the other that their father had worked a miracle, by his blessing miraculously multiplying the wine. When Henry heard this he said to them:

"Children, this is not my doing. God has permitted this pure company to reap the benefit of their good faith, and has given them to drink both spiritually and temporarily."

Once, when Henry was preaching at Cologne, one of his spiritual children who had but lately joined the Friends of God, listening in rapt attention, saw the face of the preacher transfigured in ravishing brightness. Three times during the sermon the man saw this happen, and each time it became in splendour like a radiant sun. More wonderful still, the face of the friar became translucent like a crystal mirror, so that this beginner in the spiritual life saw himself reflected in it; which sight gave him great consolation and confirmed him in his new life.

CHAPTER XXI

THE REWARD

FRIAR HENRY had grown old, and as one by one the friends on whose help and sympathy he had leaned preceded him to God, he learnt the meaning of the gradually deepening isolation which comes with advancing years. This growing sense of loneliness may be glimpsed in a wistful little note he wrote to Sister Elsbeth Stagel when her own increasing infirmities prevented her from any longer acting as his scribe.

My dear daughter, if God has used me to foretell the crosses that he has had in store for you, this has been a cruel trial for me also; for now I no longer have anyone to help me in my enterprises with the loving zeal that you were accustomed to show when you were well. I have fervently begged God to cure you if it was his holy will; and as I was not heard, I grew almost vexed with him, and told him that I would write no more books, and that I would cease my morning hymn of praise if he did not restore you to health. While my soul was tossed about by this small inward storm, I went to my oratory, and as I was wrestling in prayer my senses forsook me. I seemed to see a band of angels coming towards me singing a celestial canticle for my consolation, for they knew how sad I was. After a while they asked me why I was grieved and why I did not sing with them. I told them that my heart was troubled because it was not God's will to hear my prayer for you. At this they begged me to be at peace again, and not to act as I was doing since God had sent these crosses for your good. They told me that the cross you are now carrying will bring you precious graces in this world and in the next a magnificent reward. So be patient, my child, as I try to be, and see in this affliction simply a noble gift from God.

For many years he had preached high perfection and to the best of his powers he had practised what he preached:

In the path of renunciation there are some who wish to attach themselves to God the sovereign Good, in accordance with the impulses of their sensitive nature; as it were like animals by instinct, making no effort of mind or will. This is to serve God in a way that is unworthy of him, since man does not live nor act by instinct, but rather by intelligence and will, by reason, choice, and love. He who serves God as a man should serve him treads his natural inclinations underfoot, and is moved always and only by love. He turns aside from what is destined for his own use to consecrate it to the honour of God. "My God," he says, "it is for your honour and not for my own gratification that I wake and sleep, work and suffer; it is not for myself but for you alone that I renounce the world and its vanities."

There was once a disciple of the Eternal Wisdom who, wishing to lead a perfect life, was taken in vision to a school of learned doctors, masters of the spiritual life; and when he asked what science they intended teaching him he received this answer: "Here people are taught to die to themselves and to

158

renounce themselves in all things." Then said the disciple: "I will remain here so that I may live in more perfect peace. Here I will have a cell and, so that I may not inconvenience anyone, I will provide myself with all that I need." "No! No!" replied the master, "you must think of nothing but to renounce yourself in God, and be persuaded that the less you do the more you will advance. The more you detach yourself from yourself, the more you die to your own will, the more the divine wisdom will teach you."

To have many ambitions, to make projects and plans in the way of perfection as if we were charged with the direction of God himself, is to act contrary to true wisdom. To act in accordance with our own wills, our senses, our judgements, our natural inclinations, our pleasure, is to follow the path of blind ignorance. In this way we place ourselves at a distance from perfection, for that is acquired by self-renunciation, by dying to ourselves, losing ourselves, abandoning ourselves as though we were of no more importance than a little dust which has neither desire nor will of its own, but is carried by the will of God wherever it shall seem good to his divine majesty.

In an ever truer, deeper sense his prayer became:

Do with me, O my Jesus, in everything what is most in accordance with your supreme honour and glory. I will praise you with every breath I take until my last; and when as death draws near my voice is silenced, I will that every movement of my body —each several heartbeat—shall continue my song of praise. Grant that the sigh with which my soul leaves my body shall cry to you: "Holy! Holy! Holy! Lord God of hosts!" And when my body shall have returned to the dust from whence it came, O mighty God, grant that each grain of this dust may still hymn your praise. Winds of heaven, carry it into the wide deserts, into the upper air, even to the throne of God himself, and there until the world's end let it still sing "Holy! Holy! Holy!"

Death was preoccupying the friar, for to a dying spiritual son he wrote:

Rejoice, because your beautiful soul which is a simple being, is going to leave this narrow and miserable prison in order to fly, free and without obstacle to its eternal beatitude. Our Lord has said: "Without death, no man can see me." Death often brings fear and anguish; many tremble at its approach because many in their lifetime have not rehearsed their death hour; they can remember many sins and wasted years; they realise the terrible debt they owe to God, and so they cannot take courage.

But to you, my dear friend, I will give a counsel which I have taken from the sacred scripture, from Truth itself: If you have faults with which to reproach yourself, and of necessity this must be so, for few live in innocence and free from taint of sin, yet be not afraid at the coming of death, but arm yourself with the sacraments of Holy Church; have always before your eyes an image of Christ crucified. Look on this image, clasp it tight, hide yourself with confidence and humility in the bleeding wounds of his immense mercy; beg him to wash all your sins in these cruel wounds, in so far as his honour and glory and your own needs may require in your passage from life. Then be calm and joyful, for your sins will be washed away and you can face death courageously and without fear. Believe me, for I speak according to the faith of Holy Church which cannot be deceived. . . .

So, my dear son, raise your heart, your hands, your eyes towards heaven, and greet your heavenly country lovingly; submit your will to God's will and good pleasure and break with every earthly tie. . . .

We know very little about Friar Henry's last years, for his lovely life was so perfectly Dominican that his brethren did not think to keep an account of it. Even miracles and ecstasies seemed just a part of this life, so ordinary and yet so perfect. When he knew that his happy death was not far off, as the time of his homecoming drew nearer, his mind became more and more filled with thoughts of heaven. Sometimes he hunted up old manuscripts, some of the mystic poetry of his youth, and his eye would light on passages, inexpressibly beautiful to us, but to him, with his ever deepening, widening knowledge and realisation of the reality, no more, as his master Saint Thomas Aquinas expresses it, than a little straw. He went back to those first love raptures of his youth, when he unlocked the *breosthorde* in the *Little Book of Eternal Wisdom*. What a poor shadow it was of what he now understood.

My son, fear nothing, because he who is with me cannot perish. Lift your eyes to heaven and contemplate the glory, the light, which I have destined for those who here below have been afflicted, persecuted and crucified for love of me. This blessed city is resplendent with gold and precious stones, it shines with crystal, and is redolent of the scent of lilies, roses and all the flowers of the eternal spring. Here are the glorious thrones from which the rebel angels were driven. These I have destined for afflicted souls, my dearly loved spouses.

The saints now reigning there are full of love for you, they are awaiting your coming with impatience, they long for your presence and they never cease to intercede to God for you. They rejoice in your crosses, and they superabound with happiness when, following in their footsteps, you bear them courageously. How they glory in their shining scars, with what joy they recall the bleeding wounds which for love of me they received during their lifetime. Therefore they rejoice to see you in the midst of pain and suffering; abandoned, yet always strong and victorious. Be very sure that they love you more than the father and mother who gave you life. The love of the saints is greater than any family tie. How sweet then will be their companionship.

Happy the soul who is predestined to glory. The unveiled contemplation of the truths revealed by faith, promised by hope, are the dowry and bridal jewels which I give to my elect in heaven; it is the peaceful and assured possession of all that you so greatly love and desire. The halo, the special crown, which I am preparing for them is the glory of their works and sufferings. I surround them with a glory which is the light of my pure essence and the impenetrable depths of my divinity. It will be as though they were plunged in an ocean of sweetness. By love they are founded on me; they are so transformed in me that they can no longer will otherwise than as I will. In a word, even as God is happy by nature so are they happy by grace.

Forget for a time your afflictions and crosses; contemplate in silence these shadows and hidden clouds of paradise; and in seeing the glory of the saints strengthen your own soul, saying to it: "Where is the confusion which once weighed down these pure hearts?" No longer are their heads humbly bent, their eyes are no longer fixed on the ground. Where is their soul-agony, their crushing poverty, their groanings, their bitter tears, their wounds, the gnawing tooth of those who hated them, their inward sadness, their dereliction; all their sufferings which forced from them your cry of sorrow: "My God! My God!

Why hast thou forsaken me?" Look, O blessed ones, all your sufferings, your crosses, your human shrinking from pain; all have vanished in the twinkling of an eye. There is no more need for you to flee the malice of the world, to hide yourselves in caverns, in narrow cells; you now rejoice eternally in the beatitude of the saints, and in the joy of your triumph, you sing to God the glorious canticle: "Benediction, honour, power, strength, brightness, wisdom, thanksgiving, to our God for ever."

My son, often call to mind the glory of the saints who have preceded you, and you will forget all your own sorrows, you will no longer despair of your salvation. Looking at the way in which I treat my servants, you must understand the difference between my friendship and that of the world. The world also has its weariness and its sufferings, but even when my friends are too blind and besotted to perceive it, certain it is that, in virtue of my justice, every man who follows his own disorderly ways becomes his own executioner. He dies in despair and is punished in hell fire. My friends, on the other hand, suffer it is true many trials and crosses; but they live joyously in the hope of glory; they rejoice in peace of heart and tranquillity of spirit, and are happier in the midst of their afflictions than worldlings are with all their temporal pleasures and false peace.

At last the end came. On January the twenty-fifth, having received the last sacraments, with eyes raised to heaven, Friar Henry departed this life, and his happy soul winged its way to God. We know no more of his death than the letter of farewell which he wrote to one of his spiritual daughters:

My dearly loved daughter,

God desires and demands that pure souls carry within themselves the sign-manual of our Saviour Jesus Christ. Is it not written in the Canticle of Canticles, "Carry me as a seal on thy heart"? So every lover of the divinity ought to impress on her soul many images which should inflame her piety, many heavenly thoughts, so that her heart may always be on fire with the love of Christ Jesus.

The safest way to reach true love of God is surely to keep before our eyes the continual remembrance of him, to think and speak of him often, to nourish ourselves with his truth, to long after him and to have no other intention than that of pleasing him alone.

Let us keep our eyes ever fixed on God; let our hearts be ever open to his inspirations, so that our whole mind and being attaches itself lovingly to him. When we have the misfortune to offend him let us appease his displeasure by our prayer; when he hides himself let us seek him and give ourselves no rest until we have found him. And when we have found him, let us hold him so strongly that always, in act and repose, in joy and in work, the name of Jesus will shine like a precious jewel on our hearts; let all our speech be of nothing but Jesus. Let us think of him with such burning love while we wake, that the thought of him remains with us also in our sleep; so that with the Prophet we can say: "O God Eternal! O Wisdom most sweet! How delightful you are to the soul who seeks you, and who sighs after you only."

Take this to heart, my daughter; continual remembrance of Jesus and continual prayer to him is the crown of all spiritual exercises, and all our efforts should tend to this goal. Are the Blessed in heaven doing any other thing than contemplating God, loving him and praising him always? So, the more lovingly we fix our hearts on our Lord who is the eternal Wisdom, the more we contemplate him, the more we hold fast to him with all the powers of our soul, the more perfectly we shall rejoice both in this life and in the next. Let the remembrance of Saint Paul encourage us and animate us in our struggle. This holy apostle carried the name of his divine master so deeply engraven in the inmost depths of his affections that at the moment of his martyrdom his severed head thrice pronounced the name of Jesus. And Saint Ignatius martyr, when the executioner asked him why he repeated over and over again the name of Jesus, made answer: "It is because I carry it graven in letters of gold on my heart." And after my death they found that he had spoken the truth.

So, my gentle daughter, I come to an end of my letter; and since you ask me to place my hand on my heart over the place where the name of Jesus is graven, and so bless you before I die, I will not refuse you this consolation. Full of confidence in the mercy of Jesus Christ, I place my hand on my breast, and after having touched the mark left there by Jesus himself, I bless you; you and all my spiritual children who are consecrated to Jesus and Mary.

And now, my father and my brother, this labour of love

is ended, your book is finished; and in spirit I make the *venia* at your feet, begging you to forgive its many shortcomings. And if in what I have written there is anything which is pleasing to you, I pray you, father, to bless me also in the name of him you loved so well.

SUMMARY OF EVENTS OF
BLESSED HENRY SUSO'S LIFE

BIBLIOGRAPHY

The Life of Blessed Henry Suso, by Himself. Translated from the original German by Thomas Francis Knox, Priest of the Oratory. (Burns and Oates, 1913.)

The Little Book of the Eternal Wisdom. Translated from the German by Richard Raby. (Richardson and Son, London, 1852.)

The English Dominicans, by Fr. Bede Jarrett, O.P. (Burns and Oates, 1921.)

Etudes sur les Temps primitifs de L'Ordre de Saint Dominique, par le R. P. Danzas. (Henri Ourin, Libraire-éditeur, Poictiers, 1873.)

Œuvres du B. Henri Suso de l'Ordre des Frères Prêcheurs, traduites par E. Cartier; Librairie du Poussielgue. (Rusand, Paris, 1856.)

La Vie Mystique d'un Monastère du Dominicaines au Moyen Age, d'après la Chronique de Töss, par Jeanne Ancelet-Hustache; Librairie Academique. (Perrin et Cie, Libraires-éditeurs, Paris, 1926.)

Officium B. Mariae Virginis juxta Ritum Sac. Ord. Pred., Father Angeli Dominici Ancarani, O.P. (Typis Josephi Salviucci, Romae, 1844.)

Retraite Mystique tirée des Œuvres du B. Henri Suso, par R. Zeller. (Librairie de l'Art Catholique, 6 Place de Saint Sulpice, Paris, 1924.)

B. Henry Suso of the Order of Preachers, by a Member of the same Order. (Office of the *Irish Rosary,* Dublin, 1899.)

La Spiritualité Chrétienne, P. Pourrat, le Moyen Age, vol 2. (Gabalda, Paris, 1928.)

La Spiritualité Mediévale, par Felix Vernet. (Bloud et Gay, Paris, 1929.)

Germany, S. Baring Gould and Arthur Gilman, Story of Nations Series. (Fisher Unwin, 1906.)

A Book of the Rhine from Cleve to Mainz, S. Baring Gould. (Methuen, 1906.)

Hymns of Ter Steegen, Suso and Others, by Frances Bevan. (James Nisbet, 1904.)

See also *Catholic Encyclopædia, Catholic Dictionary,* and other books of reference.